ordinary people extraordinary power

John Eckhardt

CHARISMA
HOUSE

Most CHARISMA HOUSE BOOK GROUP products are available at special quantity discounts for bulk purchase for sales promotions, premiums, fund-raising, and educational needs. For details, write Charisma House Book Group, 600 Rinehart Road, Lake Mary, Florida 32746, or telephone (407) 333-0600.

ORDINARY PEOPLE, EXTRAORDINARY POWER by John Eckhardt
Published by Charisma House
Charisma Media/Charisma House Book Group
600 Rinehart Road
Lake Mary, Florida 32746
www.strangbookgroup.com

Cover design by Justin Evans and Bill Johnson
Design Director: Bill Johnson

Library of Congress Cataloging-in-Publication Data:

Eckhardt, John, 1957-
  Ordinary people, extraordinary power / by John Eckhardt. -- 1st ed.
     p. cm.
  Includes bibliographical references (p.   ).
  ISBN 978-1-61638-166-0
  1. Apostolate (Christian theology) I. Title.
  BV601.2.E36 2010
  262'.72--dc22

                              2010027915

E-book ISBN: 978-1-61638-264-3

This publication is translated in Spanish under the title *Gente común,
poder extraordinario*, copyright © 2010 by John Eckhardt, published by
Casa Creación, a Strang Company. All rights reserved.

11 12 13 14 — 9 8 7 6 5 4 3 2
Printed in the United States of America

CONTENTS

DEVELOPING *an* APOSTOLIC CULTURE

E VERY PERSON IS AFFECTED BY CULTURE. *CULTURE* IS defined as "the attitudes and behaviors that are characteristic of a particular social group or organization." A culture is a way of life of a group of people—the behaviors, beliefs, values, and symbols that they accept, generally without thinking about them. Each of these is passed along by communication and imitation from one generation to the next.

What you believe changes your culture.

An apostolic culture is simply the ways, beliefs, behaviors, and values of a *sent* people. I have seen a definite change in the culture of our church since we embraced the apostolic ministry. I am not implying that our previous way of doing things was wrong, but that our way of thinking and doing has changed for the better. The culture of the people of God also changed dramatically from the old covenant to the new covenant church. The apostles brought a change to the way the people of God lived. What they believed changed their culture.

What you believe changes your culture. Different cultures have different belief systems. Your beliefs dramatically affect the way you live and do things. The Protestant Reformation brought a dramatic change to the culture of the people who embraced it. It changed their way of living and worship. When you embrace new truth and revelation, your culture will change. Many today are embracing the truth of the apostolic ministry. Churches that embrace this truth will see a change in their culture.

The nation of Israel had a distinct culture. They lived differently from the nations and were punished when they tried to adapt the pagan cultures around them. They were called to be a special people with a special culture. The arrival of the new covenant saw many Gentiles coming into the church. The challenge to the early apostles was how to bring in the nations without requiring them to be circumcised and keep the Law of Moses. This was settled at the Council of Jerusalem in Acts 15.

The Gentiles were not required to become Jews. The culture was changing. The nation of Israel had unfortunately adopted many traditions that were not a part of God's Law that had affected their culture. They had a culture of "tradition" that had replaced much of God's Word. Their "culture" no longer represented what God intended. The apostles came to bring a new culture. The new culture would be one of love and service through the Holy Spirit.

Apostles are pioneers. They challenge culture that does not represent the kingdom of God. They preach and teach the culture of the kingdom of God. The kingdom includes love, humility, power, authority, and service. The kingdom is spiritual and can only be accessed and lived in by the power of the Holy Spirit. Apostles are ministers of the Spirit and minister in the power of the Spirit. The greatest change in culture came in the change from the Law to the new covenant through the ministry of the apostles.

The CULTURE *of the* KINGDOM

John the Baptist announced the arrival of the kingdom to Israel. His message was a challenge to Israel to repent. Jesus preached the same message and sent the Twelve to do the same. The Twelve were only sent to the lost sheep of the house of Israel. Israel was about to experience the arrival of the kingdom.

The kingdom is simply the rule or domain of God. Israel was commanded through the prophets to submit to this rule throughout its history. Israel refused to submit to this rule and even asked for an earthly king during the days of Samuel. This was tantamount to a rejection of the rule of the King.

The time had now come for God to exercise His covenant rule over Israel. Those who would repent would come under the rule through salvation and the Spirit. Those who rebelled against this rule would be judged. Jesus would baptize with the Holy Ghost (salvation) and fire (judgment). The result of Israel coming under the rule of God would be salvation to the nations (Isa. 60).

The apostle Peter reiterated this theme on the Day of Pentecost. He quoted from the prophecy of Joel, which speaks of the outpouring of the Holy Spirit and of blood, fire, and vapor of smoke (judgment). The remnant of Israel who believed the gospel was saved, and the unbelievers were judged.

Entrance into the kingdom was not based on physical descent from Abraham. Spiritual birth is necessary for entrance into the kingdom. This is because the kingdom is spiritual not physical. The Holy Spirit's work is necessary for entrance. The new birth and Spirit baptism is needed to enter and operate in the kingdom.

A church with an apostolic culture will empower believers to demonstrate the kingdom.

The kingdom does not come with observation. It is not a physical or carnal kingdom. Many in Israel missed the kingdom because they were looking for the wrong thing. The kingdom is not of this world. The kingdom is not meat and drink (Rom. 14:17). The kingdom is spiritual, and it is for spiritual people.

The apostles were sent to preach and demonstrate the kingdom. Jesus told the Pharisees that the expelling of demons was a sign of the arrival of the kingdom (Matt. 12:28). He cast out demons by the Holy Spirit. He imparted power and authority to the apostles, who were empowered to demonstrate the kingdom through healing and deliverance.

An apostolic culture is a kingdom culture. It is a culture of power and the Holy Spirit. The apostles ministered in power. Paul came in the demonstration of power and the Spirit. A church with an apostolic culture will empower believers to demonstrate the kingdom. Some of this is done through impartation. Apostolic leaders will impart power and authority to the members. Believers need to be activated to heal, deliver, prophesy, and preach. They must be activated to demonstrate the kingdom.

> Now concerning spiritual gifts, brethren, I would not have you ignorant.
>
> —1 CORINTHIANS 12:1

> Follow after charity, and desire spiritual gifts, but rather that ye may prophesy.
>
> —1 CORINTHIANS 14:1

Paul had to teach the saints in Corinth about spiritual gifts. Prophecy is one of the major aspects of the Spirit realm. The apostle never told them to stop these manifestations but to operate in love with knowledge. They were told to covet the gift of prophecy and to desire spiritual gifts. This is apostolic culture. An apostolic leader will encourage the people to live and operate in the Spirit. Living under

4

the rule of the King will include hearing His voice and speaking His mind through prophecy.

> Ye also, as lively stones, are built up a spiritual house, an holy priesthood, to offer up spiritual sacrifices, acceptable to God by Jesus Christ.
>
> —1 Peter 2:5

The church is a spiritual house consisting of spiritual people. The saints offer up spiritual sacrifices and worship God in the Spirit. The saints walk in the Spirit, live in the Spirit, pray in the Spirit, and sing in the Spirit. The kingdom is spiritual and is accessed and lived in by spiritual people. Apostles and all people with various ministry gifts are called to develop and lead other spiritual people.

The apostolic culture is a spiritual culture for spiritual people. Prayer, fasting, worship, healing, the Word, deliverance, prophecy, and spiritual gifts are all a part of this culture. Developing an apostolic culture is developing a culture in which spiritual people can grow and operate. It is providing an atmosphere for spiritual growth and maturity. It is providing an atmosphere for believers to exercise their spiritual gifts. The church is to be a place of training for spiritual people.

An example of this is the school of the prophets established by Samuel. Samuel provided a place for emerging prophets to be developed in their calling and gifting. Samuel established the school of the prophets and raised the prophetic level in Israel. Samuel, although a prophet, is a type of an apostle who trains and develops ministry gifts. Under Samuel's leadership, Israel's prophetics—system of teaching and training prophets—was established as a viable institution that would bring balance to the priestly and kingly ministries. Apostolic churches should develop prophetic schools to train believers in the proper flow of prophecy and prophetic ministry.

A strong apostolic culture will embrace and make room for all the gifts to flow and operate.

The presence of the Lord was so strong and powerful in Ramah, where Samuel and his company abode, that when Saul came to look for David to kill him, the Spirit of God and of prophecy came upon him, he stripped off his clothes, and he prophesied before Samuel naked, all day and night (1 Sam. 19:24). Samuel developed a strong prophetic culture in Israel. Our focus in this book is to develop a strong apostolic culture that will embrace and make room for all the gifts to flow and operate.

The apostolic culture includes worship, deliverance, teams, prophecy, ordaining, establishing, pioneering, evangelizing, prayer, teaching, helps, missions, healing, the gifts of the Spirit, holiness, impartation, and government. All of these will be discussed in this book in order to help leaders and believers move in apostolic power and authority.

Chapter 1

APOSTOLIC GOVERNMENT

Therefore also said the wisdom of God, I will send them prophets and apostles, and some of them they shall slay and persecute.

—LUKE 11:49

THERE IS NO SUBSTITUTE FOR THE APOSTLE'S MINISTRY. WE need apostles in each generation, just like we need evangelists, pastors, and teachers. When emerging apostles do not replace founding apostles, the church is in trouble. This cycle of deterioration has occurred in almost every movement and denomination. This is because of a lack of understanding concerning apostolic ministry.

Tradition has often hid the apostolic from our eyes, but this gift was never withdrawn from the church.

After the death of the early apostles, the church began to teach that the bishops (those ordained and set by the apostles) replaced the apostles as the governmental leaders of the church. The doctrine of apostolic succession was espoused by Clement of Rome. He intervened on the behalf of the presbyters of Corinth who were dismissed from the church. He ordered their reinstatement by insisting that an orderly succession of bishops be established by the apostles.

During the second century, the church came under threat from false teachings, primarily the teachings of Gnosticism. These heresies posed such a threat to the church that Irenaeus proposed the concept that the true churches must be able to trace their leaders back to the apostles. He taught that an unbroken succession of bishops founded by the apostles guaranteed the truth that a church possesses. In this way, one could differentiate true churches from the false ones led by heretics. Churches were therefore considered apostolic if they could trace their leadership back to the apostles. This is found in Irenaeus's writing *Against Heresies* (ca. 185).

The African orator Tertullian, in his treatise *On the "Prescription" of Heretics* (ca. 200), proposed that a church need only have the teaching of the apostles in order to be apostolic. In other words, there was no need to have apostolic succession in order to be a legitimate church. Clement of Alexandria (ca. 150–215) similarly proposed that a succession of doctrine rather than a succession of bishops is the most important characteristic of a true apostolic church.

> The apostle is a pioneer. This pioneering anointing causes great breakthroughs and advancement.

Cyprian, the bishop of Carthage (ca. 205–258), was perhaps one of the strongest proponents of apostolic succession. He maintained that the apostolate (the apostles) and the episcopate (the bishops) are one. In his view the bishops were the successors to the apostles, and the apostles were the bishops of old. By the mid-third century, the difference between the apostles and bishops disappeared with Cyprian.

The development of the doctrine of apostolic succession (an

unbroken line of bishops from the apostles to the present bishop of Rome) was a response to the rampant heresies being taught in the early church. This doctrine was developed to test whether a church was legitimate or not. If teachers could not trace their leadership to the apostles, they were considered false. Only the apostles and the bishops that replaced them were considered valid teachers and carriers of apostolic tradition.

This teaching further states that only ordinations conducted by the bishops were valid. This teaching rests on the false doctrine of cessationism. It rests on the false concept that bishops replaced apostles. Any teaching based on a lie is false because it rests on a false foundation. There have always been apostles in the church. Tradition has often hid them from our eyes, but this gift was never withdrawn from the church. Each generation needs apostles, prophets, evangelists, pastors, and teachers. I agree with Tertullian in stating that the doctrine of the apostles is currently available through the New Testament. Any teaching outside of it is blatantly *un*apostolic.

Paul was sent as an apostle without the laying on of the hands of the Twelve. He was an apostle by the will of God, not by the will of man. Jesus sends apostles. Although they are usually released in the local church and confirmed by prophetic ministry, their origin is from God, not man. No man has to trace his ministry directly to one of the original apostles through the laying on of hands. This would be a fruitless endeavor for the multitudes of apostles the Lord is sending today.

The apostle is a pioneer. Apostles are set in the church first. (The Greek word for "first," *proton*, means "first in time, order, or rank"— 1 Cor. 12:28.) This pioneering anointing causes great breakthroughs and advancement. New movements grow rapidly and have great momentum. This usually continues while the founding leader is alive. Movements usually try to maintain the leader's legacy by replacing the leadership with bishops, superintendents, and administrators. The movement begins to lose momentum as it becomes more administrative than apostolic. This process is called institutionalization.

The movement becomes less open to new ideas and revelation. It ceases to be a movement and becomes a monument.

Ernest B. Gentile defines *institutionalization* as "the process whereby the church of Jesus Christ becomes an established, recognized organization, a structured and highly formalized institution, often at the expense of certain spiritual factors originally thought to be important." Derek Tidball defines it as "the process by which the activities, values, experiences, and relationships of the (religious) group become formalized and stabilized so that relatively predictable behavior and more rigid organizational structures emerge." It is the name for the way in which free, spontaneous, and living (church) movements become structured and inflexible.

Inflexibility is the characteristic of an old wineskin. New wine must be poured into new wineskins. New wineskins can become old wineskins quickly after the death of the founding leaders. This has happened to almost every movement in the past. It will continue to happen unless a group can identify and raise up emerging apostles to replace the founding apostles. When the founding leaders are replaced by bishops and administrators ("governments" in 1 Cor. 12:28), the emphasis is on maintaining instead of advancing. The movement becomes less open to new ideas and revelation. It ceases to be a movement and becomes a monument.

> And in the church God has appointed first of all apostles, second prophets, third teachers, then workers of miracles, also those having gifts of healing, those able to help others,

those with gifts of administration, and those speaking in different kinds of tongues.

—1 Corinthians 12:28, niv

The New International Version of the Bible translates the Greek word *kubernesis* as "those with the gift of administration." The King James Version uses the term *governments*. The gift of administration is a very important gift to the success of any church. It is not, however, set in the church first by God. In other words, it is not intended to be the dominant anointing of the church. When the administrative gift becomes the dominant gift, the priorities of the organization become administrative instead of pioneering and advancing. The administrative gift cannot replace the apostolic gifts at the helm of the church. David Cartledge states the following:

> Where apostolic ministries are not in the church, or accessed by it, those without a ministry Gift will attempt to lead or govern the Church. The end result of this is a man-made bureaucracy. It becomes merely a democratic administration instead of a theocracy. The usual effect is the utilization of control mechanisms rather than modeled leadership. . . . The attitudes of most denominations towards apostolic leadership have tended to squeeze such gifted ministries out of their local churches. The resisted or rejected apostolic ministries have either formed independent churches, or movements that functioned without democratic or denominational restraint.

I believe that God always provides the gifts that we need in order to fulfill our destinies. It is not the will of God that movements start out with great power and momentum, only to shrivel up and die after one generation. The apostolic gift is the key to continuous advancement and momentum. There is always another generation of apostles that should be in position to replace the founding apostles.

> The church faces an unfortunate situation
> when administration takes over the apostolic,
> because the very gifts that churches need
> to advance are usually lost due to the
> organizational constraints placed upon them.

When an organization or church becomes administrative at the expense of being apostolic, apostolic gifts are often choked out. This is because apostolic gifts tend to be too progressive, pioneering, and advancing for many organizations. Some would identify this as rebellion, but usually it is a desire to keep the group moving forward and walking in present truth.

However, the church faces an unfortunate situation when administration takes over the apostolic, because the very gifts that churches need to advance are usually lost due to the organizational constraints placed upon them. This happened in the early church when bishops replaced apostles. The church became more ceremonial and traditional. The apostolic power and grace of the church in the Book of Acts was lost. The Reformation of the sixteenth century began to change this. The reformers, however, failed to restore the proper role of the apostle. Many Reformation churches kept the episcopal (bishops) form of government. We are now seeing the restoration of apostles to their proper role in the church.

APOSTLES ORDAIN BISHOPS (*or* ELDERS)

The third chapter of 1 Timothy gives the qualifications of bishops (overseers, elders). Paul is giving apostolic instruction to Timothy concerning the government of the local church. Timothy is functioning as an apostle.

Apostles are responsible for the oversight and setting of leaders in local churches. The traditional concept of bishops being over groups of churches is really an apostolic function. The teaching that bishops replaced apostles removes the role of current apostles from the church. Some have taught that the bishop is the highest office in the church. This is not true. God has set apostles first in the church. No amount of scriptural wrangling can remove them from this position in the church.

Apostles ordain and set bishops (overseers, elders) in the church. Titus was sent by Paul to ordain elders (bishops, overseers) in the church at Crete (Titus 1:5). Paul and Barnabas appointed elders (bishops, overseers) in the churches they established (Acts 14:23). In his book *The Last Apostles on Earth*, Roger Sapp states the following:

> We must recover the scriptural understanding of the apostle and the overseer, and for the sake of the Church put away the unscriptural ministry and the title of bishop. It is evident from a simple look at these passages that all or at least the vast majority of those Christian leaders who have accepted the title of bishop did not receive it from apostolic ministry and have accepted a role that usurps the role of the apostle. For present-day bishops to acknowledge this error to the churches that respect them will be difficult, but necessary, to make room for apostolic ministry to come forth. Otherwise, the "old wineskin" will not be suitable to hold the "new wine" of the Spirit that will be poured out in the days preceding the coming of the Lord. In some cases, it will not be difficult for the man of God to dispense with this title and to instruct those who look to him for leadership about the apostolic ministry over a short time. It will be for him a question of humility and love for the truth. In other cases, due to long tradition it may not be possible to do so without serious difficulties. In any case, the Lord will grant His servant grace to embrace the truth.

Chapter 2

FIRST, APOSTLES— LAST, APOSTLES

God hath set…in the church first apostles, secondarily prophets, thirdly teachers…

—1 CORINTHIANS 12:28

For I think that God hath set forth us the apostles last, as it were appointed to death: for we are made a spectacle unto the world, and to angels, and to men.

—1 CORINTHIANS 4:9

THE APOSTLE'S MINISTRY IS THE HIGHEST-RANKING MINISTRY in the church. This does not mean that an apostle has jurisdiction over every church. There are different apostles who have different spheres of influence. Apostles have different geographical regions to which they are set and sent.

The FIRST SHALL BE LAST

Although apostles are set in the church *first*, they are often treated as *last*. The rise of bishops to positions of prominence in the church coincided with the state's recognition of the church. Bishops often became more powerful than natural rulers. This began when the Roman emperor Constantine recognized Christianity as the religion of the Roman Empire. The bishop's office eventually became a position of power and prominence.

True believers and ministries cannot avoid suffering and persecution, especially apostolic ministries who minister in power and authority.

Some leaders like the use of the term *bishop* because it is recognized by the world. Apostles have always been persecuted and hated by the world's system. They know what it means to suffer and be treated as last. Many leaders are afraid to walk in true apostolic ministry because they fear rejection and persecution. Many desire honor from men rather than honor from God. Some religious leaders even receive titles such as "His Eminence" or "His Holiness." How disgusting this must be to God, because it is a manifestation of pride and arrogance. We should not think of men "above that which is written" (1 Cor. 4:6).

Many leaders don't like the idea of being treated last. Many desire to be treated first. Being treated last is hard on the flesh. The flesh hates suffering, rejection, and persecution. The flesh loves flattering titles. Leaders must be aware of the subtle trap of religious pride. True believers and ministries cannot avoid suffering and persecution, especially apostolic ministries who minister in power and authority.

TERMS *and* TITLES ARE IMPORTANT

There are many leaders today who refer to themselves as bishops who are apostles. Many are aware of it; some are not aware. The word *bishop* means "an overseer." The word *apostle* has a much broader definition and broader function. Apostles provide oversight to churches. They are also elders. The word *apostle* is a transliteration of the Greek word *apostolos* meaning "one sent forth." A sent one has a variety of functions and duties, including overseeing, planting, watering, encouraging, correcting, judging, activating, imparting, demonstrating, establishing, pioneering, mobilizing, teaching, preaching, and ordaining. Leaders who are apostles cannot limit themselves to managerial duties but must fully express the grace that is upon the apostolic office.

The same thing is true of many pastors. Pastors who are apostles need to recognize this gift and walk in it fully. Pastors cannot allow fear and tradition to hold them back. God has not set in the church first pastors, but first apostles. This is an order of ministry for the local church. Paul wrote to a local church when revealing God's order of ministry.

Some will maintain that terms are not important. Terms and words are very important. Words have definitions. Words shape our way of thinking. Apostles cannot think like pastors. Apostles must think and act like apostles. Our lack of understanding of gifts and ministries can hinder us from walking in the fullness of God's grace. We are not to be ignorant of spiritual gifts (1 Cor. 12:1).

Chapter 3

The STRATEGY of JESUS and EMERGING APOSTLES

And when he had called unto him his twelve disciples, he gave them power against unclean spirits, to cast them out, and to heal all manner of sickness and all manner of disease. Now the names of the twelve apostles are these; the first, Simon, who is called Peter, and Andrew his brother; James the son of Zebedee, and John his brother; Philip, and Bartholomew; Thomas, and Matthew the publican; James the son of Alphaeus, and Lebbaeus, whose surname was Thaddaeus; Simon the Canaanite, and Judas Iscariot, who also betrayed him. These twelve Jesus sent forth.

—MATTHEW 10:1–5

AN APOSTOLIC CULTURE WILL REQUIRE APOSTOLIC LEADER-ship. This will require the wisdom and strategy to identify and release emerging apostles and other ministry gifts.

Jesus ordained twelve that they might be with Him. Many have looked at the strategy of Jesus as a one-time, historical event. Jesus is our perfect example. He is the apostle of our profession. He is the perfect sent one. His methods and strategies reflect the wisdom of an apostle.

> The failure to discern and train emerging
> apostles often causes the next generation
> to replace the apostle's leadership with
> managers and administrators.

Jesus identified twelve apostles. Was this a one-time event or a model that modern apostles need to have? One of the failures of many apostles has been the failure to identify emerging apostles. Many apostles identify pastors to shepherd the churches that are birthed through their movements. This is not the wisdom of God for several reasons. The first reason is that the next generation of leaders also will need an apostolic anointing to continue in the momentum of the founding apostle. Jesus identified leaders that would carry His message and penetrate to the uttermost parts of the world. Apostles have the ability to break through and expand the movement begun by the founder.

God will place emerging apostles around a founding apostle. It is up to the founding apostle to discern who they are and train them. The failure to do so often causes the next generation to replace the apostle's leadership with managers and administrators. Some fellowships resort to voting in order to replace leaders. Without emerging apostles the fellowship is not in a position to advance and progress. The apostolic gifts in a church need to be recognized, encouraged, and released. This is the strategy of Jesus, and it should be our strategy today.

Joshua is a type of an emerging apostle. The Lord told Moses to encourage him. Emerging apostles need to be encouraged. They need spiritual fathers who will mentor and train them. There are many emerging apostles in the church today, and they cannot be locked into managerial positions that limit their anointing. They need to be released fully.

Timothy and Titus were emerging apostles who were trained by Paul. Emerging apostles will often be a part of the apostolic team. They will travel with an apostle and learn firsthand apostolic ministry. They will be a part of planting and establishing churches as well as ordaining ministers. Their gifts will take time to fully come forth, but through patience and maturity these gifts will be able to fully manifest.

When leaders step fully into apostolic callings, many emerging apostles will have a model to follow. Ministers will follow the models set before them. If all ministers see are bishops and pastors, this is all many will aspire to become. If they see apostles and prophets honored and received in the church, they will have a New Testament model before them. We are responsible for what we model before emerging ministries. Paul encouraged the church to follow him as he followed Christ. Paul presented a true apostolic model before the churches. He exposed false apostles and modeled the true.

OUT WITH *the* OLD MODELS—*in* WITH *the* NEW

We cannot afford to present old religious models before the church. Traditional models will not suffice. The church is built upon the foundation of apostles and prophets (Eph. 2:20). It is not built upon the foundation of bishops and pastors. This is not to say we don't need bishops (elders, overseers) and pastors. It simply means these are not foundational ministries. They are not the primary ministries of the church. When we replace foundational ministries with ministries that are not foundational, the church is in trouble.

> Paul, an apostle, (not of men, neither by man, but by Jesus Christ, and God the Father, who raised him from the dead).
> —GALATIANS 1:1

Paul always identified himself as an apostle. Apostles are called and sent by Jesus. Bishops are appointed and set by apostles. Paul knew his calling and setting was not by man. He understood the authority of his calling was given directly by the Lord. When he corrected churches, he did it based on his apostolic authority. His authority came from God and not from the church. Bishops who are set in their positions by the church are accountable to the churches that elect or appoint them. How can leaders walk in the necessary authority without the authority coming from God?

> The order of apostolic ministry is a threat to
> a pyramid type of leadership structure.

This is one of the reasons many organizations have a problem with apostles. Apostles operate in a level of power and authority that make many uncomfortable. Bishops who are apostles also walk in authority, but this authority comes from their apostolic grace. Apostles have the authority of a "sent one." They have ambassadorial authority. Authority is a distinct mark of the apostle's ministry. This authority is recognized in the spirit realm. Angels and demons recognize this authority. This authority registers in the spirits of people. Apostles are first in time, order, and rank.

Many organizations and denominations will have a hard time embracing the order of apostolic ministry because it is a threat to a pyramid type of leadership structure. When emerging apostles are raised up and released they will in turn raise up and release emerging ministries. This is a threat to control mechanisms that are set in place in many structures. Mature spiritual sons will raise up sons and daughters. There is a greater release of gifts and ministries when apostles are in place. Many emerging apostles will develop their own networks and spheres of influence.

Chapter 4

The DEPARTURE
RESTORATION *of*
APOSTOLIC MINISTRY

For I know this, that after my departing shall grievous wolves enter in among you, not sparing the flock. Also of your own selves shall men arise, speaking perverse things, to draw away disciples after them.

—ACTS 20:29–30

PAUL WARNED THE CHURCH WHAT WOULD HAPPEN AFTER his departure. Evidently the enemy could not do these things while he was present. The apostolic anointing provides a restraining influence to division and false ministry. The church is always susceptible to these attacks when the apostolic mantle departs. This happened historically with the death of the early apostles. The church drifted into tradition, ceremonialism, and heresy. This is the reason why the apostle's ministry is so needed in the church.

> And when the people saw that Moses delayed to come down
> out of the mount, the people gathered themselves together
> unto Aaron, and said unto him, Up, make us gods, which
> shall go before us; for as for this Moses, the man that brought
> us up out of the land of Egypt, we wot not what is become
> of him.
>
> —EXODUS 32:1

Moses is a type of an apostle. The people began to rebel when he departed from the camp. His presence provided a restraining influence. This is what happens when strong leadership departs. People need strong leaders. The church needs the apostolic anointing to be present. The devil will do anything in his power to remove this ministry from the church. If there are no emerging apostles to replace the founding apostle, the church tends to choose leaders after the flesh. Every Moses needs a Joshua. Every Elijah needs an Elisha. Every Paul needs a Timothy. The church cannot afford to have a void in apostolic leadership.

> Now after the death of Jehoiada came the princes of Judah,
> and made obeisance to the king. Then the king hearkened
> unto them. And they left the house of the LORD God of their
> fathers, and served groves and idols: and wrath came upon
> Judah and Jerusalem for this their trespass.
>
> —2 CHRONICLES 24:17–18

Jehoiada the priest mentored and trained the young king. He was a father to the king. He is a type of an apostolic minister. His death marked the beginning of a spiritual decline for the nation. The princes of Judah came to the king and enticed him to disobey after Jehoiada's departure. Jehoiada's presence was a restraining influence to the powers of darkness. The apostolic ministry has the power to bind. This is another reason why the devil hates this ministry. He wants it to die in the church. He has influenced the church to believe that the apostle's ministry ceased after the death of the Twelve.

Without apostles, the church is susceptible to the influence of the spirits of division and carnality.

The devil has always hated and feared the apostle's ministry. It is the most misunderstood and persecuted ministry in the church. The enemy has successfully removed this ministry in its fullness from the church through tradition and false teaching. The major lie the enemy influenced the church to accept was that bishops replaced apostles. The enemy effectively stole the role of the apostle from the church. Thank God we are presently seeing a restoration.

This is why it has been necessary to view what happened in church history after the death of the early apostles. There is always a danger when apostolic ministry departs from the church. Paul warned of wolves entering the flock. The Corinthian church became divided and sectarian after Paul's departure. The schisms in the Corinthian church were probably due to the fact that there were no strong apostolic leaders present in the church. Churches are more unified when the apostolic anointing is present. Without apostles, the church is susceptible to the influence of the spirits of division and carnality.

> Also he made a molten sea of ten cubits from brim to brim, round in compass, and five cubits the height thereof; and a line of thirty cubits did compass it round about. And under it was the similitude of oxen, which did compass it round about: ten in a cubit, compassing the sea round about. Two rows of oxen were cast, when it was cast. It stood upon twelve oxen, three looking toward the north, and three looking toward the west, and three looking toward the south, and

three looking toward the east: and the sea was set above upon them, and all their hinder parts were inward.

—2 CHRONICLES 4:2–4

The molten (brazen) sea was a type of the cleansing power of the Word. It was the basin of water that the priests washed in before they ministered in the tabernacle. It is also a type of the apostle's ministry. It rested upon a foundation of twelve oxen. Twelve is the number of government and the apostolic ministry. Oxen represent the laboring aspect of the apostolic ministry. The oxen faced every direction, representing the apostles going into all the world. The church is built upon the foundation of the apostles and prophets. The enemy desires to remove this foundation from the church.

And king Ahaz cut off the borders of the bases, and removed the laver from off them; and took down the sea from off the brasen oxen that were under it, and put it upon the pavement of stones.

—2 KINGS 16:17

King Ahaz removed the molten sea from its proper foundation. He placed it upon a pavement of stones. This is what the enemy did to the church. Church tradition has removed the church from its apostolic foundation. When apostles and prophets are not operating in the church, the church is not standing on its proper foundation. One of the ways the enemy did this is by influencing the church to believe that bishops replaced apostles. The church is not built upon the foundation of the bishops, but it is built upon the foundation of the apostles.

The church should be a nonclerical family. The separation of clergy and laity has brought much damage to the church. Bishops are sometimes referred to as "high clergy," while those ministers under them as "low clergy."

> The Christian church was a people's movement. The distinguishing mark of Christianity was not found in a clerical hierarchy but in the fact that God's Spirit came to dwell within ordinary, common people and that through them the Spirit manifested Jesus' life to the believing community and the world.
>
> —ALEXANDER STRAUCH

With the institution of the clergy came a distinction in dress. Robes, collars, staffs, and rings became the dress of bishops. Clerical dress became mandatory for those ordained as bishops. We are seeing a revival of this kind of wear among Pentecostal and Charismatic leaders who identify themselves as bishops. This is totally foreign to the early apostolic church. When the church becomes clerical, it loses the simplicity that the early apostles desired. The result is a religious caste system that elevates men to positions of power and prominence that is dangerous and carnal.

> The division of the church into clergy and laity causes the saints to invest the majority of ministry into the hands of a few.

Apostles are given for the perfecting of the saints. They are one of the five ministries given for this purpose. Apostles are called to activate believers to do the works of Jesus Christ. They are anointed to impart and stir up the gifts inside of the believers. Their position is not one of fleshly prominence. They are usually treated "last." They are driven and motivated by a commission, not by worldly fame and power. They are not clerical. In other words, they do not represent some priestly order inside the church. They know that all believers are priests.

The church must be careful not to revert back to clericalism. The reformers challenged this concept and brought reformation by exposing it as a false system. Clerical terminology can hinder the church from being a nonclerical family. The division of the church into clergy and laity causes the saints to invest the majority of ministry into the hands of a few. The fivefold ministry is given for "the perfecting the saints, for the work of the ministry" (Eph. 4:12).

A TIME *of* RESTORATION

We are presently living in a time of restoration. The Lord is restoring the order of apostolic ministry to the church. With restoration comes reformation. Adjustments and alignment to the truth is necessary in order to receive the new wine that is being released. Religious tradition is being challenged. The church is returning to New Testament terminology and truth.

Many leaders are beginning to embrace their true callings and ministries. They are being loosed from fear and tradition that has hindered them from walking in the higher callings. It is important that true apostles understand their function in order to release their gifts fully to the church. Apostles are more than bishops (overseers). They have a unique anointing to advance the church. Apostles must be free to minister in the church. They cannot be limited by false teachings and governmental structures that are not biblical. The truth will make us free.

God is also restoring prophets to their governmental positions in the church. This will not fully happen until apostles take their place. Religion and tradition has always been a hindrance to the release of the gifts of the Spirit. Apostles have the ability to activate the gifts through impartation and the prophetic word. With the restoration of apostles and prophets will come the greatest release of the power of God. We must study to show ourselves approved unto God. Ignorance will no longer be an excuse. God is opening His Word and causing us to know His secrets. We are stewards of the mysteries of God.

The new leaders the Lord is releasing must shed the old, religious garments of the past. We cannot sew a new piece of cloth on an old garment. The new anointing that God is releasing will not work with an old mentality. Remember, words represent concepts and ideas. The way we think is governed by our vocabulary. We must renew our minds according to the Word of God in order to receive what God is releasing from heaven. Holding on to the old while trying to receive the new will not work. This is like the wineskins metaphor Jesus used in Matthew 9:16–17: we cannot put new wine into old bottles.

Chapter 5

The APOSTOLIC SPIRIT—DRIVING FORCE of the CHURCH

Then said Jesus to them again, Peace be unto you: as my Father hath sent me, even so send I you. And when he had said this, he breathed on them, and saith unto them, Receive ye the Holy Ghost.

—JOHN 20:21–22

WHEN I TALK ABOUT THE APOSTOLIC, I AM ALSO REFERring to apostolic believers. All are not apostles, but all can be apostolic. The apostolic spirit is a driving force of the church, and every believer can operate to some degree in the apostolic. Apostolic leaders should develop an apostolic people. The flesh profits nothing; it is the spirit that gives life.

Our spiritual lives depend upon movement.
That which stops and stagnates will die.

The same is true concerning a local church. The direction and movement of the church is determined by the spirit of the church. The condition of the spirit will determine the mobility of the wheel. *The spirit is the fuel that releases the power that moves the church.* If the enemy can kill the spirit of a believer or a church, he can stop the church.

By *spirit* I mean "passion, drive, zeal, energy, and excitement." The spirit is that which motivates, drives, compels, and moves to action. It is that which stirs up and gives fuel to the dream, vision, or goal. Tired, discouraged, frustrated, and lazy believers are lacking the necessary spirit that moves the church. When the wheel is not turning, there is no movement. The result is stagnation. Believers and churches are meant to move. Believers are the driving force of the church. Both must move. If individual believers are not moving, the church is hindered from moving. If churches are not moving, individual believers are hindered from moving. Both need to move. We must move corporately and individually.

The spirit is what drives the church. *If your spirit is not in what you are doing, you will not be moving.* You must be excited about what you are doing. You must have energy and zeal. You must have a passion for what you desire to accomplish. The same is true concerning local churches and the entire body of Christ. People must be motivated.

Our spiritual lives depend upon movement. That which stops and stagnates will die. Churches will die if the believers stop moving. The church at large would die if it were not for church movements within the universal church. *Every move of God is a driving force in the church.*

> And he was sore athirst, and called on the LORD, and said,
> Thou hast given this great deliverance into the hand of thy
> servant: and now shall I die for thirst, and fall into the hand
> of the uncircumcised? But God clave an hollow place that

was in the jaw, and there came water thereout; and when he had drunk, his spirit came again, and he revived: wherefore he called the name thereof Enhakkore, which is in Lehi unto this day.

—JUDGES 15:18–19

Tiredness, weariness, and discouragement are deadly enemies to the believer and the local church. Samson had no strength left after defeating the Philistines. Warfare takes a lot of energy. After Samson called to the Lord, water was released. After he drank, he was revived. The Bible says, "His spirit came again."

Samson was an individual army. He represents the strength of an individual anointed by God. Although we are part of a corporate body, we are individual believers. I call an individual believer "a driving force within the church." Each believer needs to move individually. One cannot depend totally upon the movement of the corporate church.

The spirit of revival needs to be in the church. Water needs to flow continually. Believers must drink and keep their spirits strong and fervent.

How many believers do you know who have lost their spirit? They have lost their energy, strength, zeal, and enthusiasm. They have been in battles that have drained them. They no longer have the strength to fight. Their movement has stopped. They are no longer moving against the enemy. They have come to a standstill.

In Judges 15:19 we read that God clave a hollow place and out came water. I believe this is referring to local churches that are being hollowed out to release water that brings the spirit back to the believer. Believers can drink and see their spirit come again. Their dreams, visions, energy, and zeal are restored. The wheels are once again being set in motion. Believers must be refreshed and revived on a continual basis. The spirit of revival needs to be in the church. Water needs to flow continually. Believers must drink and keep their spirits strong and fervent.

One of the important ingredients of motivated believers is an apostolic spirit. The Holy Spirit is an *apostolic spirit* because He is a *sent* Spirit. A *sent* people must have a *sent* spirit. People who are sent should have a sense of purpose and destiny. They should be driven by a commission. When people have an apostolic spirit, they are driven to execute and carry out the purposes of God.

Apostolic believers are motivated by a sense of calling and sending. I call the apostolic spirit "the driving force of the church." These believers are not just led; they are driven. They are driven to fulfill the Great Commission. They have the zeal of the Lord. They are concerned with finishing.

An apostolic company of believers is a movement within the church. They provide movement and impetus to the church. They help release spiritual momentum. They are a movement within a movement. They are driven and motivated by an apostolic spirit. This apostolic spirit is what moves the church.

The present-day apostolic movement is helping to propel the church. The release of modern-day apostles is fueling this movement. The revelation of the apostolic ministry is coming from heaven into all the earth. Last-day apostles are on the rise. They are impacting their territories and nations with apostolic doctrine and power. This is causing a new driving force to hit the church. The result of the restoration of apostolic ministry is a release of an apostolic company of believers. They in turn become a driving force within the church universal.

I call these believers *proton believers. Proton* is the Greek word for "first" in 1 Corinthians 12:28. It represents a pioneering, breakthrough anointing. Proton believers are breakthrough believers. They are first in time, order, or rank. They are the first to embrace new moves of God. They are the first to embrace and preach a truth that is being restored to the church. They are the result of restoration.

Proton believers will expand the borders of the church. This will move the church into new regions and territories, both naturally and spiritually. It will move the church beyond past limitations and boundaries and help us to go where we have not gone before. It mobilizes the church. This is driven by a pioneering, breakthrough spirit.

There is no limit to the power that can be released through the local church. Apostolic churches can have an impetus and momentum that move them to affect nations.

Apostolic churches are a driving force within the church universal. The Antioch church is an example of this. The church at Antioch became a hub for apostolic missions throughout the world. From Antioch, apostolic teams were sent out to plant strategic churches in Asia and Europe. The churches of Phillipi, Thessalonica, Corinth, and Ephesus were all planted as a result of Antioch's *sending.*

The church at Antioch became a movement within a movement. They moved in apostolic power and grace to expand the kingdom of God. They sacrificed and released key ministries to do this. They ministered to the Lord, prayed, and fasted to impact nations. There is no limit to the power that can be released through the local church. Apostolic churches can have an impetus and momentum that move them to affect nations.

These churches are strong because they have an apostolic spirit. They have within their structure strong ministries. They have leadership with a strong spirit. The spirit of these churches is strong because they have believers and leaders with strong spirits.

Antioch churches are *spiritual hubs.* A hub is a center of activity. Wheels rotate around a hub. Apostolic churches become pivotal places of divine activity. They are places of movement and action.

MOVEMENT WITHIN
the LOCAL CHURCH

Not only can a local church be a driving force the church universal, but there are also movers within the local church. Each of these believers needs to move in order for the church to move and progress. The following groups are driving forces within the church:

1. *Prayer*—Intercession and fervent prayer is a movement within the church. Each local church needs a prayer movement. When believers move in prayer, the church will advance and break through.

2. *Praise and worship*—Churches need strong praise and worship teams to move the church into strong praise and worship. The praise and worship of the local church should always be advancing and progressing.

3. *Evangelism*—Evangelism and outreach is an important part of the expanding and growth of the church. Evangelists and evangelistic teams need to continually move in the power of the Holy Spirit.

4. *Prophetic ministry*—Prophets and prophetic teams need to minister the Word of the Lord. This releases the church into its destiny and purpose. It is an important driving force within the church.

5. *Deliverance*—Driving out evil spirits helps the church to move forward and progress because it opens the way for people to possess the land.

6. *Teaching*—The teaching of the Word of God is important because it helps the church move into the understanding of Scripture. Teachers and teaching teams need to move in knowledge, understanding, and revelation.

7. *Missions*—This is a part of the apostolic mandate of the church. This wheel needs to be moving in order to impact and touch nations. The sending of apostolic teams is an integral part of the apostolic church.

8. *Pastoral ministry*—The release of pastors and pastoral teams within the local church is an important part of watching over and maintaining the saints. This ministry needs to be continually moving and expanding.

The spirits of prayer, praise, worship, evangelism, prophecy, deliverance, teaching, and missions need to be strong in the local church. The apostolic and pastoral spirits must also be strong. This will keep these wheels moving and keep the church moving.

ACTS—*a* BOOK *of* MOVEMENT

The Book of Acts is a book of movement. *Acts* means "movement." The following synonyms for the word *movement* were taken from J. R. Rodale: "motion, action, activity, stir, move, *acts*, actions, proceedings, doings, goings on, comings and goings." The Acts of the Apostles records the movements of the apostles.

Movement also means "progress, progression, advance, advancement, or forward motion." The Book of Acts records the progress of the church.

From its beginning in Jerusalem to the uttermost parts of the earth, the church is a movement. The present-day church is part of a worldwide movement that began two thousand years ago. The church is a wheel. It is in motion. God's will is for the church to continue to progress and advance.

Every movement within the church helps it to progress and advance. *Progress* means "furtherance, breakthrough, and improvement." With each movement, there is a corresponding breakthrough. In order for the church to continue breaking through, the wheels within the wheel of the church must move.

The present-day restoration of apostles is a movement that will help the church move fully into its purposes and destiny.

The apostolic spirit is the driving force of the church. The present-day apostolic movement is driven by the apostolic spirit. The Holy Spirit is first and foremost an *apostolic* Spirit because He is a *sent* Spirit. This is what pushes and drives the church toward the fulfillment of the Great Commission.

Most movements within the church are apostolic in nature because the apostolic spirit is a pioneering spirit. Apostles initiate new movements. They help push the church into new places. Apostolic movements sweep across the earth, breathing new life into the church, to release impetus and momentum. They cause an acceleration to come to the church.

The present-day restoration of apostles is a movement that will help the church move fully into its purposes and destiny. This wheel is moving within the church. It is a wheel (restoration of apostles) in the middle of the wheel (the church). It is at the core of what God is doing today.

The middle represents the core or center of something. There are movements that are in the middle of what God is doing in the earth. We need to locate the movements that are central to what is happening in the purpose of God. We should desire to be in the middle of what God is doing. We want to be in the center of God's will.

Chapter 6

The PROTON BELIEVER

And God hath set some in the church, *first [proton] apostles,*
secondarily prophets, thirdly teachers…
 —1 Corinthians 12:28, emphasis added

ARE YOU A *PROTON* BELIEVER? ARE YOU A PART OF A *PROTON* company of believers? Are you a part of a *proton* church? As has been stated in previous chapters, *proton* is the Greek word for "first" mentioned in 1 Corinthians 12:28. It means "firstly in time, place, order, or importance." It also means "before, at the beginning, chiefly, first of all." God desires a proton people. *Apostolic people are proton people.* This is the culture of the apostolic.

> **Proton believers draw their life and**
> **strength by and from the Sender. They are**
> **not men-pleasers but God-pleasers.**

It was never the will of God just to have apostles. God's intention is to have an apostolic company of believers. Apostolic churches and apostolic believers will be at the forefront of what God is doing. When believers have an apostolic spirit, they will be proton believers.

When the apostolic spirit is present within the church, we will see a company of believers who walk in apostolic power. They will manifest certain characteristics that set them apart.

Proton believers are sent ones.

> Then said Jesus to them again, Peace be unto you: as my Father hath *sent* me, even so send I you.
> —JOHN 20:21, EMPHASIS ADDED

They have an awareness of being sent. Jesus is the Sender. They live by the Sender (John 6:57). They draw their life and strength by and from the Sender. They desire to do the will of the Sender (John 6:38). They do the works of sent ones (John 5:36). Their works bear witness that they have been sent. They judge as sent ones (John 5:30). Their motivation is to do the things that please the Sender (John 8:29). They are not men-pleasers but God-pleasers.

Proton believers are pioneers—the first.

What does it mean to be first? What are the characteristics of those who are first? *First* refers to responsibility. It refers to inheritance and blessing. It refers to authority. It is a privilege to be first. There are advantages to being first. It is a favored position.

> Those who are first are pioneers. Proton believers are pioneers. They are trailblazers. Proton believers are a remnant people who set the tone and direction for the church.
> —JIM HODGES

These believers are pathfinders. Synonyms for *pioneer* include "pathfinder," "trailblazer," "explorer," "forerunner," "predecessor," and "innovator." *To pioneer* means "to set in motion, start the ball rolling, take the first step, take the initiative, break the ice, lead the way, blaze the trail, institute, inaugurate, find, establish, set up, lay the first stone, lay the foundation, introduce, launch, or usher in." These are things that proton believers do.

There are different areas and ways in which one can be first:

- FIRST in *power* represents a potentate.

- FIRST in *authority* represents a ruler or a leader.

- FIRST in *rank* represents a captain or a general.

- FIRST in *knowledge* represents a valedictorian or a doctor.

- FIRST in *time* represents a pioneer.

- FIRST in *lineage* represents a patriarch.

- FIRST in *revelation* represents a prophetic people.

- FIRST in *suffering* represents a martyr.

- FIRST in *believing* represents the firstfruits of them that believe.

- FIRST in *receiving* represents the firstfruits of them that receive.

- FIRST in *blessing* represents the firstborn.

- FIRST in *possessing* represents a Joshua generation.

- FIRST in *breakthrough* represents a people of new levels.

Proton believers are breakthrough people!

A breakthrough is a significant or sudden advance or development. It is also an act or instance of removing or surpassing an obstruction or restriction. Proton believers initiate breakthrough into new regions and territories, both naturally and spiritually. They are cutting-edge believers. They are on the forefront of what God is doing in the earth. If a trail is not there, they will make one. They follow the paths that others have already opened and make new paths when necessary. They are people of faith who believe and act on what they believe.

As pioneers, they are both *dependent* and *independent.* They are independent from the control of men. They are very dependent upon the Holy Spirit and His direction. They refuse to be controlled by the opinions of men. They are not controlled by family or friends. They are not controlled by religious organizations that refuse to move with change. They hate witchcraft, slavery, and control. They would rather obey God than man (Acts 5:29). They rely upon the blessing and power of God. They recognize that without God they can do nothing.

Proton believers are often considered crazy.

> For whether we be beside ourselves, it is to God: or whether we be sober, it is for your cause.
>
> —2 CORINTHIANS 5:13

There is a reason behind the proton believer's "madness." Pioneers are often accused of being crazy. They don't make sense to natural men. They operate beyond what is considered reasonable. They go beyond the limitations of natural reason. They often try what is "unreasonable" but succeed. They are not afraid of failure. They operate with the spirit of faith. They are not controlled by fear. They are not afraid to try new things. They are not afraid to preach new truths. If they fail, it is no reflection on them because they are not afraid of losing their reputation. Their reputation does not come before obeying God.

Proton believers are looked to by others as models of kingdom living. They release the blueprints that men can see to build their lives and ministries according to the heavenly pattern.

The proton believers of the previous move may not be the proton believers of the present move. *It takes a great deal of strength to be a proton believer.* Much energy is expended in the advancing of the purposes of God. Some believers, after expending much strength in previous moves, would rather rest and enjoy the benefits of what they have already achieved. They have a hard time pressing into new battles in order to conquer new territory.

We derive our word *prototype* from the Greek word *proton*. A prototype is a model. It is a standard. Proton believers set new standards. They raise up models for future generations to follow. A prototype is a paradigm. It is a pattern. *Proton believers are pattern believers. Proton churches are pattern churches.* A pattern is something that can be duplicated. Proton believers live a lifestyle that can be duplicated in other places. They are looked to by others as models of kingdom living. They release the blueprints that men can see to build their lives and ministries according to the heavenly pattern.

David was a proton believer. He released a pattern of worship. Abraham gave us a pattern concerning faith. Samuel released a pattern concerning the prophetic. Joshua gives a pattern of warfare. Elijah gives a pattern of prayer. Daniel gives us a pattern for dreams and visions. Jesus is our pattern for being sons and daughters of God. He is the perfect pattern of heaven on Earth. Paul is a pattern apostle.

Proton believers are people of conviction. They are people of passion and zeal.

They are not double minded. They know what they believe and are convinced it is from God. This gives them the ability to overcome persecution that may arise for the Word's sake. Conviction is certainty, assurance, trust, position, persuasion, faith, creed, or doctrine. Proton believers know what they believe and are convinced of its validity based on the Word of God.

Preaching without conviction does not
move anyone. Preaching with conviction
can change a city, region, or nation.

Some people have a problem with people who have conviction. To some, they are too strong and may even be considered dogmatic. Dogma is a firm belief or conviction. The world believes in tolerance. In other words, tolerate any opinion even though it may be incorrect. Anyone with strong opinions is considered intolerant. Preachers who preach strongly are considered intolerant. John the Baptist would have been considered intolerant. Elijah would have been considered intolerant. Jesus made some strong statements, and He would be considered intolerant by many. We can be *people of conviction* and still minister in love. Conviction does not necessarily equate with being prejudiced or bigoted.

People of conviction change things. Reformers have conviction. Great men and women are people of conviction. Paul was a man of conviction. He was convinced of the truth of the gospel he preached. Stephen died because of his conviction. The early apostles died for their convictions. These men turned the world upside down and influenced their generation. Preaching without conviction does not move anyone. Preaching with conviction can change a city, region, or nation. John Knox was a man of conviction. His messages struck fear in the heart of tyrants and kings, and his preaching shook Scotland.

Proton believers minister with passion.

Passion is compelling emotion. It is strong enthusiasm. It is a strong desire for something. Proton believers preach with passion. They worship and minister with passion. Jesus was consumed with zeal (John 2:17, NIV). He was passionate about His Father's house. Proton believers are passionate about the house of the Lord.

Proton believers are extreme.

Extreme is going well beyond the ordinary or average. It means "exceedingly great in degree." It means "to be radical." Proton believers do not compromise to avoid persecution. They do not preach balance at the expense of truth. They believe in going all the way. To them, compromise is not an option. *Extreme* means "exceptional, extraordinary, maximum, and complete."

Proton believers are people of courage.

These two characteristics are necessary to be a proton believer. It takes courage and boldness to be at the forefront of what God is doing. They keep their boldness in spite of opposition and persecution. To be *bold* means to be intrepid, fearless, and daring. Proton believers are bold to preach new truth. They are bold to try new things. "The righteous are as bold as a lion" (Prov. 28:1, NIV). The lion is a symbol of the apostolic ministry. It is a picture of courage and boldness. It represents fearlessness. The lion was the symbol of Judah. *Judah* means "praise." *Proton believers are bold in praise.* They are also bold in dealing with demons.

Proton believers are people of faith.

> By faith Abraham, when he was called to go out into a place
> which he should after receive for an inheritance, obeyed; and
> he went out, not knowing whither he went.
>
> —Hebrews 11:8

Abraham is a type of a proton believer. He left his home in obedience to the word of God, not knowing where he was going. He had to move out by faith. Sometimes proton believers are moving out to a destination unknown. All they know is that they have heard from God. Apostolic believers carry a spirit of faith (2 Cor. 4:13).

**Grace enables proton believers to do extraordinary
things: preach, teach, prophesy, cast out devils,
heal the sick, pray, worship, and give.**

Pioneers have to believe. They must launch out in faith, not knowing sometimes where they are going. To some they may appear to be reckless or foolish, but they have heard from heaven. They leave their places of comfort and security to receive a promised inheritance. Abraham became the father of faith to all who would believe. He left a pattern for future generations to follow, "which in other ages was not made known unto the sons of men, as it is now revealed unto his holy apostles and prophets by the Spirit" (Eph. 3:5).

Proton believers are people of great grace.

> As every man hath received the gift, even so minister the
> same one to another, as good stewards of the manifold grace
> of God.
>
> —1 Peter 4:10

Apostolic ministry is a ministry of great grace (Acts 4:33). Proton believers are stewards of the manifold grace of God. They come behind in no gift, waiting for the coming of the Lord (1 Cor. 1:7). We call this *mega-grace*. *Mega* is the Greek word for "large." It means "large quantities or things that are extraordinary examples of their kind."

Proton believers are gifted.

These gifts are the result of grace. These gifts are for blessing others. Proton believers are a blessing wherever they go. They bring salvation, healing, and deliverance to multitudes. Grace enables them to do extraordinary things. This is *apostolic grace*: grace to preach, teach, prophesy, cast out devils, heal the sick, pray, worship, and give. This is also *manifold grace*. *Manifold* is defined as "many kinds, numerous, and varied." It means having numerous different parts, features, or forms. Proton believers are not one-dimensional. They are multidimensional. They are multifaceted. They operate in different operations and manifestations of the Spirit.

Proton believers are people of revelation.

Apostolic ministry is a ministry of revelation. Proton believers have insight into truth that was hidden in previous generations. They walk in truth that was not known in previous ages. Revelations are mysteries revealed. Proton believers are stewards of the mysteries of God (1 Cor. 4:1). They dispense these mysteries throughout the earth through their preaching and teaching. They understand divine secrets. They have the privilege of understanding the mysteries of the kingdom of God. Revelation is insight. It is spiritual perception. It means an unveiling. Things that were veiled or hidden are unveiled. People who live by revelation are not limited by their natural understanding. They understand the invisible realm. They see what others cannot see. They operate on a higher level.

Proton believers are people of purpose and destiny.

Proton believers have insight into the plans and purposes of God. They are driven by purpose. They have definite goals. They know where they are going and have a strategy to get there. Purpose is intention, aim, objective, expectation, vision, dream, hope, or desire. *Purpose* means "determination, resolution, resolve, firmness, single-mindedness, persistence or perseverance." People of purpose are devoted to finishing a commission. They are people of zeal. Nothing can turn them away from their purpose. They are driven to finish. Opposition or setback does not deter them. Nothing moves them from finishing their course (Acts 20:24).

Proton believers are people of perseverance.

> Truly the signs of an apostle were wrought among you in all patience, in signs, and wonders, and mighty deeds.
> —2 CORINTHIANS 12:12

Patience (perseverance) is a mark of true apostolic ministry. They persevere in spite of hardship and danger. They are patient in tribulation. They rejoice in tribulation. They glory in their infirmities. When they are weak, they are strong. They are focused on fulfilling their commission and do not allow trials to deter them. They understand that tests and trials come with the territory. They do not think it strange concerning fiery trials. They trust in the grace of God to sustain them. *To persevere* means "to persist in pursuing something in spite of obstacles or opposition." Proton believers are persistent. They do not give up. They have spiritual tenacity. They have a spiritual resolve and determination to continue in spite of the attacks of darkness.

Proton believers are people of sacrifice.

They are willing to make sacrifices in order to advance the purposes of God. They make financial sacrifices and sacrifices with their time. They lay down their lives. They are willing to lose in order to gain. *To sacrifice* means "to make an offering." Proton believers offer themselves as a sacrifice. They offer their time, money, and life to the purposes of God. No price is too high to pay. Jesus is their example. He offered Himself to God as a sweet-smelling sacrifice acceptable to God.

Apostolic ministry is a ministry of sacrifice. Those who are first are expected to make sacrifices. Parents make sacrifices for their children. Pioneers make tremendous sacrifices for advancement and progress. Abraham was willing to sacrifice his son and became an example of righteousness by faith. Jesus gave His life as the firstborn Son of God. The sacrifices of proton believers bring blessings unto many. We are all blessed by the sacrifices of those who have gone first.

Proton believers are laborers.

The apostolic anointing is a laboring anointing. Jesus said, "The harvest is plentiful but the workers are few" (Matt. 9:37, NIV.) We are commanded to pray to the Lord of the harvest that He would send forth laborers into His harvest (Matt. 9:38). To "send forth" is an apostolic term. After sending the Twelve, Jesus identified them as workmen (Matt. 10:10). The word translated "workmen" is the same Greek word for "laborer." Apostles and apostolic people have the ability to labor under pressure. They are tireless in executing the will of God. They labor in spite of persecution and hindrances from the enemy. They are hard workers.

Proton believers do not "burn out." They have a grace to labor.

Their strength is in the Lord. When they are weak, they are strong (2 Cor. 12:10). They work by supernatural power that is given by grace. Their bodies are quickened by the Holy Spirit. They live with supernatural energy that gives them strength to work hard. Epaphras labored in prayer (Col. 4:12). Paul stated that he himself labored more abundantly than all the apostles (1 Cor. 15:10). He was able to labor

47

because of grace. He planted churches, trained new believers, traveled extensively, and wrote much of the New Testament. He did all of this in spite of shipwrecks, stonings, beatings, imprisonment, and being buffeted by a messenger of Satan. Proton believers have a grace to labor in spite of what they have to encounter.

Proton believers are people of warfare.

> (For the weapons of our warfare are not carnal, but mighty through God to the pulling down of strong holds;) Casting down imaginations, and every high thing that exalteth itself against the knowledge of God, and bringing into captivity every thought to the obedience of Christ.
>
> —2 CORINTHIANS 10:4–5

The Greek word for "warfare" is *strateia*, which means "apostolic career." The Greek word for "imaginations" is *logismos*, which means "logic" or "mind-set." They are not afraid to fight for what they believe. They understand that they wrestle not against flesh and blood but against principalities and powers. They contend with the powers of darkness that are set against the expansion of the kingdom of God.

Proton believers are pioneers.

Those who are first (pioneers) must fight. They always experience and come up against opposition. Innovators are usually opposed and misunderstood. They must fight the status quo and those who are resistant to change. Pioneers fight. Generals conduct warfare. Fathers should fight for their families. Those who are first must guard and protect. They advance into new territory and subdue giants. The first generation that went into Canaan had to fight. Saul, Israel's first king, had to fight the Philistines.

Proton believers decree and issue official
declarations on behalf of the King. This authority
is recognized in the spirit realm. Principalities
and powers cannot ignore this authority.
Their authority is legal and is official.

The enemy always opposes and fights those who are first. He recognizes their importance and influence. He tries to hinder and stop them. He knows that after them, more are coming. He persecuted the first church in Jerusalem. He killed all of the first apostles. He hates those who are first. This is why those who are first are people of warfare.

Proton believers challenge the mind-sets that prevent the church from obeying the truth.

They war against the strongholds in the minds of men that keep them in ignorance and darkness. Ignorance is the enemy of proton believers. They are committed to the manifestation of the truth. They contend with the carnal inclinations of the flesh. They confront and war against the carnality that prevents men from understanding spiritual matters. They desire the meat of the Word. They desire to walk in the deeper truths of the Word. They desire to go on to perfection.

Proton believers war with the supernatural weapons of love, faith, hope, prayer, fasting, praise, and the Word.

They cannot become bitter because of false accusation or opposition. They bless their enemies. They must forgive and cannot take opposition personally. Their warfare is not against flesh and blood. They understand who the enemy is.

Proton believers are people of change.

They are agents of change. They initiate and activate change by their preaching and prophetic declarations.

Proton believers are people of transition.

They are people who have transitioned out of the old into the new. They are moving. They do not live on the victories of the past. They enjoy the victories of the past but recognize that there is new ground and territory to conquer. Transition is movement. Proton believers are moving toward a goal. They are not stagnant. *To transition* means "to shift." Proton believers shift into the prevailing position that God is releasing. They shift into the *new move* of the Holy Spirit. There is a shift taking place around the world today. The church is shifting from the pastoral to the apostolic. Proton believers are in the forefront of this shift. Proton believers are able to shift from old paradigms into new paradigms.

Proton believers are people of power and authority.

They exercise power and authority over demons. They root out, pull down, destroy, throw down, build, and plant (Jer. 1:10). They have been sent *and* set. They depend upon the authority of the Sender. Proton believers speak and act on the behalf of the Sender. They are ambassadors. They are delegates of the King. Proton believers decree and issue official declarations on behalf of the King. This authority is recognized in the spirit realm. Principalities and powers cannot ignore this authority. Their authority is legal and is official. It is not illegitimate. Proton believers have the authority to act on behalf of the King. They are officials of the kingdom.

Proton believers will preach what is in the Word, regardless of what tradition or religion says.

Official means "to be duly authorized." It means "to be rightful, lawful, legitimate, legal, certified, licensed, or valid." This authority is sanctioned by heaven. It is, therefore, recognized by both angels and demons. This authority also affects the human spirit. People are impacted when they come into contact with proton believers.

Proton believers prophesy, preach, teach, and minister with authority and power.

Power is force. Power causes impact. Power is ability or capacity. It is energy, vigor, or capacity. It is might and strength. These are characteristics of proton believers. There is an ability to break through and change territories and nations. They have the authority and power to execute the will and purposes of God. The will of God must be executed. *To execute* means "to carry out, accomplish, or perform." The duties of the apostolic ministry must be carried out by those who are graced to execute them. This is a supernatural ability to get the job done.

Proton believers are people of the Word.

They base what they do on the Word of God. They do not allow tradition to make the Word of God of no effect. They will preach what is in the Word, regardless of what tradition or religion says. They are motivated and driven by what they believe the Word of God teaches.

Proton believers are governed by the Word of God.

The Word sets their perimeters. To be on the forefront does not mean being "out of control." Proton believers must stay within the boundaries of the Word. The Word limits and sets free. To operate in authority, one must be under authority. Proton believers are submitted to the authority of the Word.

They reject the philosophies that prevent men from obeying the Word. They allow no one to spoil them through philosophy and vain deceit after the tradition of men (Col. 2:8). Proton believers are committed to rediscovering the truths of the Word that have been lost or rejected through tradition and unbelief. They are people of restoration. They believe in current truth. They are committed to restored truth that is rediscovered in the Word of God.

Proton believers are people of new strategies.

Those who go first must have a strategy. You cannot go into uncharted territory without a strategy. Proton believers develop new strategies. They do not depend upon strategies of the past. Their strategies are based on revelation. Each generation must receive and work out its own strategies. Old rules and methods may no longer apply. Old limitations are no longer in place.

Proton believers are leaders.

They are the leaders of their generation. Strategy involves generalship. Generals are commanders. They are first in rank, and first in rank implies leadership. They have the ability to gather and mobilize. They have the ability to lead into battle and win. They have expertise in tactics and logistics. They give direction and guidance. They have power and influence. They motivate and mobilize people to accomplish a goal. Strategies are for leaders. Leaders set strategy and implement it according to a plan. Great leaders are known for great strategy. Proton believers are the leaders of the new things that God is releasing.

Proton believers are strategic people.

Proton churches are strategic churches. *Strategic* means "important and crucial." It means "key or vital." God always has strategic people and strategic places. God is a God of strategy. Everything God does is strategic. He moves through strategic people, churches, and places. Apostles and apostolic people are both strategic to the purposes of God. They are important and vital to the plans of heaven. That which is first is important.

Every field has those who are first. Again, generals are first in rank. Pioneers are first in time. Patriarchs are first in lineage. Presidents are first in government. Valedictorians are first in their class. They are first in knowledge. These individuals are recognized as important in their respective fields.

Proton believers have goals, and they have the strategies to accomplish those goals.

They are leaders. They are first in strategy. They develop pioneering strategies to do new things. They are cutting-edge leaders with pioneering technologies. Pioneering strategies are needed to break through into new regions and territories. They are needed to pioneer new moves and new revelations.

Proton believers have a team mentality.

Apostolic ministry is team ministry. Jesus gathered a team to be with Him. Barnabas and Paul (and later Silas and Paul) were apostolic teams released from Antioch. Jesus sent the disciples out two by two (Luke 10:1).

Proton believers understand the power and dynamics of the corporate anointing. They understand the strength of corporate worship and corporate prayer. The church in the Book of Acts saw tremendous breakthroughs as a result of corporate prayer (Acts 4:31). The entire church was mobilized and moving in the same direction. Unity is the strength of proton believers.

> Proton believers know the power of praise. They
> are radical when it comes to praise. They release
> praise as a weapon against the powers of hell.

The team concept is found throughout the Word of God. Moses and Aaron, Moses and Joshua, Elijah and Elisha, Paul and Timothy, and Jesus and the disciples are all examples of teams. Samuel raised up prophetic teams. He is a type of apostolic ministry. David mobilized teams of priests and Levites to minister before the Ark of the Covenant.

Although proton believers may have different ministries and anointings, they understand the importance of working together in teams. There are apostolic teams, prophetic teams, evangelistic teams, deliverance teams, prayer teams, praise and worship teams, teaching teams, and pastoral teams.

Proton believers are mobilized people.

They have been activated in their gifts, and they are ready to work and minister. With so many people being released, it is understandable why there is wisdom in developing and releasing teams.

Proton believers are people of praise.

> Now after the death of Joshua it came to pass, that the children of Israel asked the LORD, saying, Who shall go up for us against the Canaanites first, to fight against them? And the LORD said, Judah shall go up: behold, I have delivered the land into his hand.
>
> —JUDGES 1:1–2

The tribe of Judah was a proton tribe. They were sent first. *Judah* means "praise." Proton believers know the power of praise. They are radical when it comes to praise. They release praise as a weapon against the powers of hell. They have their hand in the neck of the enemy (Gen. 49:8). Proton believers have a scepter of authority (Gen. 49:10).

Proton people love to sing new songs (Ps. 96:1). New moves always release new songs. There is a freshness in the praise and worship of proton believers. They are the first to move into new songs and new sounds. They play skillfully with a loud noise (Ps. 33:3). When God is doing a new thing, He releases new songs.

Proton believers are people of new things.

They serve God in newness of spirit (Rom. 7:6).

> Behold, the former things are come to pass, and new things do I declare: before they spring forth I tell you of them. Sing unto the LORD a new song, and his praise from the end of the earth, ye that go down to the sea, and all that is therein; the isles, and the inhabitants thereof.
>
> —ISAIAH 42:9–10

These are the identifying marks of proton believers: pioneering, breakthrough, authority, power, revelation, boldness, grace, conviction, warfare, prayer, praise, courage, purpose, destiny, perseverance, strategy, teamwork, the Word, change, transition, and newness. *God loves a proton people!*

Chapter 7

TRANSITIONING *a* CHURCH *Into the* APOSTOLIC

Christ loved the church and gave himself up for her to make her holy, cleansing her by the washing with water through the word, and to present her to himself as a radiant church, without stain or wrinkle or any other blemish, but holy and blameless.

—EPHESIANS 5:25–27, NIV

A S I TRAVEL AROUND THE WORLD MINISTERING IN THE area of the restoration of apostolic ministry, I am finding many leaders desiring to transition from a pastoral calling to an apostolic calling. They are realizing that they have a greater calling than just being a pastor of a church. They know they need to make a transition but do not know the steps they need to take to do it successfully.

This book is written to help leaders make the transition. It will provide wisdom to help churches transition and develop an apostolic culture. Our experience in Crusaders Church of Chicago helps me to help others in making the transition. We have seen our church make this transition with tremendous results.

RESTORATION REFORMATION

We are currently seeing another reformation in the church at large. We are also experiencing restoration. God is restoring the ministries of apostle and prophet within the local church. As a result of this restoration, we need to reform and change the way we build churches. Unfortunately, tradition has robbed much of the church from receiving and believing in apostles. The three ministries most churches receive and believe in are the pastor, teacher, and evangelist. Most of the leaders in the local church accept the title and function of "pastor" when it comes to starting and overseeing churches. Most churches have been built around the pastoral anointing. The pastoral anointing has been the dominant anointing of the local church.

Most leaders have been trained to think pastorally. Bible schools and seminaries train leaders to be pastors and administrators. This is because many Bible schools are staffed by former pastors, teachers, and administrators. These leaders generally operate with a pastoral mind-set. Our churches have been built to meet the needs of the members, and most members expect it to remain this way. It is common to see a leader serve as a pastor of a church for many years. We commend the many pastors who have faithfully served in local churches for many years.

There is, however, a shift taking place throughout the earth. Many leaders are sensing an apostolic call. Many of them are presently pastors of local works. They are sensing and responding to a higher calling. Many have been operating in a pastoral context for so long that they do not know how to make the transition.

This book is designed to help leaders shift into the prevailing position that God is establishing upon the earth. This prevailing position is apostolic. Not only must leaders shift, but entire congregations must also shift. If leaders shift without their congregations shifting, they will leave the membership behind. The result will be a gap between the leaders and the members. If leaders do not shift, the congregations will not be able to shift. If both leadership and congregations shift, you will see a quantum leap in anointing and power.

When the leadership of the church shifts, the entire church will shift as well. Our desire should be to raise up an apostolic company of believers who all have a sense of being sent. The entire church needs to shift into this dimension. The church in the Book of Acts was first and foremost an *apostolic church*. The book is called *Acts of the Apostles*. The apostles ministered in apostolic power and turned the known world upside down.

This book will help pastors place themselves and their churches into a position to shift. It will give them the characteristics and ingredients of an apostolic ministry, including the steps they need to take to strengthen the local work. When a leader shifts into an apostolic position, the demands upon this anointing will increase substantially. We are not attempting to make everyone an apostle, but we do believe that every leader can be apostolic.

You cannot fulfill an apostolic calling with a
pastoral mind-set. A pastoral mind-set will limit
a leader and confine him to the local church.

As mentioned earlier, we are now living in a time of restoration. God is restoring the apostolic ministry. He is also restoring the revelation of this ministry. Many leaders who have been called into this ministry are seeing for the first time who they really are. They are no longer looking at themselves through the eyes of tradition. There is a shift in leadership taking place throughout the earth. Many leaders are hearing the call to shift and transition from being pastoral to becoming apostolic. There are many leaders who are apostles, but they are so bound by the tradition of being pastors that they do not know or see it.

You cannot fulfill an apostolic calling with a pastoral mind-set. A pastoral mind-set will limit a leader and confine him to the local church. Many leaders are beginning to realize that what they have been doing is apostolic, yet they have been limited by a pastoral mentality. They are now being challenged to fully embrace and walk in an apostolic call. I pray this book will open the eyes of many to their true calling so that they will respond and begin to walk in it. Apostolic leaders are also shepherds, and in no way am I neglecting the pastoral ministry. An apostolic framework will include but is not limited to pastors.

Seasons *of* Transition

Transition is defined as "movement; passage; or change from one position, state, or stage to another." It is a period during which such changes take place. Apostolic times are seasons of transition. Change is difficult for leaders who are comfortable with the status quo. Change requires commitment and humility. It also requires listening to the voice of God and following His leading.

To shift means "to transfer from one place, position, or person to another." It means "to put aside and be replaced by another." The greatest transition and shift in the Bible occurred between the Old and New Testaments. Jesus came to bring a shift between Old Testament Judaism and the New Testament (Christian) church. Many were not ready for the shift. Many fought against it. Those who shifted were blessed. Those who did not missed the blessing.

Leaders cannot afford to be ignorant of this restoration move of the Holy Spirit. Leaders must come into the knowledge of this current shift in the church. There is an apostolic mandate for many senior pastors. Unless these leaders come into the knowledge of this change, many will remain locked in a pastoral mode the rest of their lives. This will drain them of their joy, zeal, and vitality. Many are already sensing this and know that they must change in order to keep their enthusiasm for ministry.

Local churches must release these leaders to function in an apostolic call. Many leaders cannot move fully into the ministry God has for them because the leadership structure is not in place for them to be released. Many of these leaders are not free to move out into a larger ministry because of the restraint placed upon them through tradition. If an apostolic leader cannot leave the church for even a short period of time, then something is wrong. We should not build churches to depend upon one leader.

If leaders do not move into new positions, they will die spiritually within the four walls of the church. They will experience dryness, and their ministries will become routine. They will be unhappy and unsatisfied, even though it may look successful on the outside. On the inside, these ministers will feel empty. Many are afraid to transition because they think the church is dependent upon them.

> If an apostolic leader cannot leave the church for even a short period of time, then something is wrong. We should not build churches to depend upon one leader.

Many have built their churches to depend upon them and have found satisfaction in feeling indispensable. Now they are locked into a pastoral mode and are unable to move out, even though the Holy Spirit is leading them to do so. Many are afraid to leave their churches for any period of time and operate in a call to the larger body of Christ.

If most leaders would leave their churches for any period of time to do apostolic ministry, their churches would fall apart. This is not to imply that an apostle must give up a local work completely. It simply means that you must be able to obey God without losing what you have spent years building. You must build your ministry in such a way that you are not tied down but are free to obey God.

If churches do not release their leaders to move into a higher level of ministry, they will frustrate the leaders and grieve the Holy Spirit. Churches must be set free from what they think their leaders should be and do. We will see more leaders raised up who will not fit the traditional concept of "pastor." They cannot be locked into a position and place because of the expectations and demands of the people. Both leaders and churches must be free to operate in the higher callings and gifts of God.

The church will not become obsolete in a changing world. God will upgrade our methods, structure, and models to be able to impact our world.

Leaders, you cannot be afraid to make this shift. Fear will paralyze you and prevent you from possessing your inheritance. There are many of you who are even afraid of the term *apostle*. Some of you are comfortable with *pastor* because it is accepted and respected by most of the church and the community. You cannot be afraid of the terms God has given us in His Word. You have received Holy Ghost–inspired words to understand spiritual things (1 Cor. 2:13).

PARADIGM UPGRADE

We are living in another time of great shifting. God is realigning and restructuring the church. After years of building churches one way, we are all of a sudden confronted with a new and better way. In order for churches to shift, there must be a shift in leadership. The leaders of the church must make the shift into a new order of ministry. This is a *paradigm shift*. A paradigm is an example serving as a model. The model for building churches is changing.

Even the world knows the importance of shifting. Economies must shift to continue to grow. We have shifted from the industrial age to the communication age. Nations and economies that do not shift are left behind and become obsolete. Obsolescence is a terrible price to pay for not being willing to change. *Obsolete* is defined as "being of a discarded or an outmoded type." It means "to be out-of-date."

Methods can become obsolete. Models and structures can become obsolete. Organizations can become obsolete. When something becomes obsolete, it is no longer relevant. We are living in a world of change. The church will not become obsolete in a changing world. God will upgrade our methods, structure, and models to be able to impact our world.

This change for many may seem like a quantum jump. This is a sudden and significant change, advance, or increase. The shift from a pastoral to an apostolic role is a significant jump. However, by the grace of God, we can make the transition. Quantum jumps have happened throughout the history of the church. God often moves us into greater levels of ministry quickly and suddenly. These shifts are happening quickly around the world. God has been preparing the church for this jump. It is now time to take the leap and move into another level of anointing and power.

Chapter 8

CHALLENGING TRADITION

You nullify the word of God for the sake of your tradition.
—MATTHEW 15:6, NIV

IN ORDER TO MOVE INTO THIS NEW POSITION, WE ARE CHAL-lenging some of the traditional ways we have been taught. Restoration will always challenge our theology and adjust our way of thinking. The New Testament pattern of planting and building churches is being restored. In the Book of Acts, churches were planted by apostles and apostolic teams, *not* pastors. There is not one place in the New Testament that shows a church being planted by a pastor. The planting and building of churches is an apostolic function, not a pastoral one. It takes a pioneering anointing to plant churches. There is a grace upon apostles and apostolic teams to pioneer and break through. Because much of the church does not believe in present-day apostles, many leaders who perform apostolic work have been iden-tified as pastors. This is the title we place upon the leaders of most local churches.

Because of this restoration of the ministry of apostle, we must redefine the role and function of the pastor. With *restoration* comes *reformation*. This will be painful for many who resist change and cannot see any other way of doing ministry. We must challenge the concept of a church having only one pastor. There can be many people with pastoral callings within a congregation. As churches grow and disciples multiply, there is a need for many pastors to help shepherd the flock. Pastors are not mentioned among the three governmental offices of the church (1 Cor. 12:28). Yet, we have made the office of pastor the governmental office of the church.

> God hath set…in the church, first apostles, secondarily prophets, thirdly teachers…
>
> —1 Corinthians 12:28

Apostles, prophets, and teachers are the governmental gifts of the church. These anointings have been left out of the government of most local churches and have been replaced by the office of pastor. This is unscriptural and grieves the Holy Spirit. We have violated God's order and have suffered for it. The result is that we have many pastors trying to build and plant churches that require an apostolic anointing, and they do not have the necessary grace to succeed. The result is many small, weak churches that cannot properly manifest the power of the kingdom of God.

On the other hand, we have seen many leaders identified as pastors who have planted and built strong churches, which are apostolic functions. We have locked many of them into a pastoral role and not allowed them to function in the calling of an apostle. The church has been pastoral for so long that we have not known any other way. But God is challenging the church to change and come in line with His purpose.

THE APOSTOLIC GIFT EMPOWERS MULTITUDES *of* PASTORS

Once apostles are released, thousands of pastors will be released within the local church to help shepherd the flock. The cell group movement illustrates this point. The need for cell groups was birthed out of the need for believers to receive and be a part of ministry in a small group context. We have called these leaders *cell leaders* or *care leaders*, when in reality they are doing the work of a pastor. They are watching over a small group. Our tradition has not allowed them to be called *pastors* because that title is reserved for the leader of the local church. It is possible to release thousands of pastors in this way. These are people gifted with a genuine call to shepherd the sheep. They have a grace to touch the flock and minister to them in a unique way. They counsel, love, heal, reach out, protect, and rescue the sheep. This should not be limited to one person or a pastoral staff of a few. God does not give associate pastors or assistant pastors, but pastors (Eph. 4:11).

Apostles will embrace and release pastors to help shepherd the flock, because they understand the need for them to be able to shepherd large numbers of people who are being harvested. They are not fearful and intimidated by other anointings.

In Crusaders Church, we have ordained and released pastors who have caring gifts to minister to the flock. They are not in the governing presbytery of the church. They understand their pastoral gifts in relationship to the apostolic covering of the church. They are submitted to the vision of the church and do not try to form their own flock. They are shepherds within the flock. They are free to minister to the flock and are not burdened with administrative and financial duties that most pastors are concerned with. They are not bound by the traditional concept of the pastor. They do not have to be the head of the local church to function as pastors. They can fulfill their God-given duty of shepherding the sheep. They have been set free from tradition to bless the people. Churches must expand their pastoral base by acknowledging and releasing those with the gift of pastoral leadership.

Many pastors will be afraid to recognize and release pastoral gifts in their congregation for fear of these individuals gathering small flocks around them. Pastors have inherited a system that creates suspicion and distrust. This is why leaders must develop an apostolic mind-set. Apostles are also shepherds. When Jesus taught His disciples how to minister to the needs of the people, He described the multitudes as being sheep without a shepherd. But He sent them out as twelve apostles, not twelve pastors (Matt. 9:36; 10:2–5; 10:42). Apostles have the ability to shepherd multitudes. They will have more of a rancher style of leadership. They will embrace and release pastors to help shepherd the flock, because they understand the need for them to be able to shepherd large numbers of people who are being harvested. They are not fearful and intimidated by other anointings. They are secure in their gifting, and their authority is respected by others.

In addition to pastors, churches should also have prophets (1 Cor. 14:29). Our concept of having one pastor over a church has severely limited the other gifts from being released. This pyramid style of church government often shuts out the other gifts from fully functioning. This is especially true in the case of prophets. There are many people sitting in our churches with prophetic gifts.

Leaders who have a pastoral mentality will often be afraid to release prophets. The pastoral gifting is not anointed to release gifts like the apostle's anointing. This is why our churches must become more apostolic. The pastoral anointing is also needed, but it cannot be the dominant anointing. The apostolic anointing must become the dominant anointing. It is placed in the church *first* by God. The apostle has a grace to release other gifts. As our churches migrate toward an apostolic mentality, we will see the release of many gifts—including that of the prophets.

The apostolic anointing should be the primary, foundational anointing of the church. We are first and foremost sent by the risen Lord. As sent ones, we have a purpose and mission.

Many pastors think in terms of safety and protection. The apostle thinks in terms of expansion and progression. This does not make one better than the other. They are both needed in the church. The problem occurs when the pastoral anointing becomes the dominant anointing of the local church. The church then thinks only in terms of safety and protection and often eliminates the other gifts that may be more radical and progressive. The result is the church becoming too pastoral at the expense of not being apostolic and prophetic. On the other hand, churches that are apostolic can be so without the expense of losing the pastoral. The apostolic ministry has the capacity to embrace the other gifts. The apostolic mentality is anointed by God to think largely and to incorporate all the gifts of God. The pastoral mind is not anointed in the same way.

EMBRACING *an* APOSTOLIC MENTALITY

This is why leaders need to embrace an apostolic mentality and dimension if they are to have the capacity to embrace and walk in all that God is releasing. Staying in a pastoral mode will hinder them from partaking fully in what is being made available during this season of restoration. Making the transition will not eliminate the pastoral anointing in the local church. On the contrary, it will release it more by releasing others to function in their pastoral gifts.

The word *first* in reference to apostles in 1 Corinthians 12:28 is the Greek word *proton,* meaning "first in time, order, or rank." *First* also means "principle or primary." The apostolic anointing should be the primary, foundational anointing of the church. We are first and foremost sent by the risen Lord. As sent ones, we have a purpose and mission. The commission Jesus gave the church is an apostolic commission. This is why the apostolic anointing should be the dominant anointing of the church.

The word *proton* is also the root of the word *prototype.* We need to see prototype churches built that will be models for the twenty-first century. These churches will have strong apostolic leadership. They will also have strong prophetic, teaching, pastoral, and evangelistic gifts. They will be fully functional churches. They will come behind in no gift (1 Cor. 1:7). This will result from leaders making the necessary shift and transition into apostolic ministry. This will position the church to receive the new wine that God is pouring into the new wineskins that are being created around the world. This will happen once the church recognizes and walks in God's divine order of ministry for the church.

Chapter 9

BUILDING ANTIOCH CHURCHES—TEACHERS

Now there were in the church that was at Antioch certain prophets and teachers.

—ACTS 13:1

THE ANTIOCH CHURCH IS THE MODEL APOSTOLIC CHURCH in the Book of Acts. It is a sending church and gives us the pattern of strong presbyteries and apostolic teams. The apostolic revolves around the concept of sending and being sent. From Antioch, the team of Barnabas and Paul (and later Silas and Paul) was released for an apostolic work throughout the known world. Antioch became an apostolic mission base that affected nations and planted strategic churches. It is our prototype church that models for us an effective base that serves to establish the kingdom of God in regions beyond.

The account of the release of the first apostolic team is found in Acts 13. As certain prophets and teachers ministered to the Lord and fasted, the Holy Ghost instructed them to release Barnabas and Paul. This apostolic team was birthed and released out of an atmosphere of the prophetic and teaching gifts. These are two of the areas that need to be strengthened in the local church in order to transition into a strong apostolic position.

The TEACHING GIFT

If a church is to transition into an apostolic position, the minds of the people must be renewed. People must receive a revelation of the present plans and purposes of God. Apostles and prophets have a unique anointing to reveal to the church the mysteries of God. They are stewards of the mysteries of God (1 Cor. 4:1). They help reveal to the church the mysteries that were hidden in previous ages (Eph. 3:5). Once people understand the plans and purposes of the Lord, they will be able to walk in them. People need to understand what apostolic ministry is and how it relates to what the Lord is presently doing in the church.

This is called *re-laying apostolic foundations.* The previous foundation of the church will not be sufficient to build and expand upon. A new foundation of truth must be laid in the church. A foundation based on present truth must be put into believers. When Paul visited Ephesus, he had to lay a new foundation within the believers. The previous foundation laid by Apollos was insufficient (Acts 19:1–7). Apollos's revelation was not sufficient, knowing only the baptism of John. This is the case with many existing churches. The present foundation is insufficient to build what the Lord is revealing today.

For years in our local church in Chicago, we have taught on the subject of apostolic ministry. The more we taught, the more revelation the Lord granted us.

> …and unto you that hear shall more be given.
>
> —MARK 4:24

We were faithful to teach what we knew in the beginning, and God granted us more understanding as we continued to teach.

At the time, there were not many books on the subject of apostles and apostolic ministry. Most believed and taught that this ministry was not for the present-day church. Now we have more material available than ever before. Jonathan David's book *Apostolic Strategies Affecting Nations* is a must to read and study. David Cannistraci's book *Apostles and the Emerging Apostolic Movement* and Roger Sapp's book *The Last Apostles on Earth* are also invaluable resource tools for today's church. I have written several books on this subject, including *Moving in the Apostolic, The Ministry Anointing of the Apostle, Fifty Truths Concerning Apostolic Ministry, The Apostolic Church, Presbyteries and Apostolic Teams,* and *Apostolic Ministry (a 50 Lesson Bible Course).* I highly recommend that leaders read these books and begin to teach the truths to their congregations.

> The church does not revolve around the
> ministry of one leader, but around a team of
> leaders with apostolic vision that comes from
> a revelation of proper church government.

One reason that teaching is so important is that people will not be able to make the shift unless they shift their minds. Most people have been trained to think pastorally. They have a parish mentality. They join a church and spend all of their time and energy maintaining the church and getting their needs met. All the resources for most local churches, both natural and spiritual, go into maintaining the local church and meeting the needs of the members. People come each Sunday to hear preaching and teaching and receive healing and encouragement. The pastor is expected to preach, counsel, marry, bury, and oversee the administration of the church. This is the way most believers have been trained, and this is their understanding of the church.

The apostolic mentality is quite different. The leader is released by the people into an apostolic function to the larger body of Christ and to geographical regions outside of the local church. The local church takes on the burden of apostolic ministry to regions beyond and to the nations. The people realize that the church is about more than just having their needs met and that it is also about touching others with the resources that God has given us by His grace. More ministries are released to meet this burden and fulfill this vision. The church does not revolve around the ministry of one leader but around a team of leaders with apostolic vision that comes from a revelation of proper church government. The vision to plant churches and send out teams is birthed in the heart of the people by seeing this pattern in the Word of God.

In an apostolic church, the governing gifts of apostles, prophets, and teachers are set in place. The gifts of pastoring and the outreach gifts of evangelism are released. The people learn to draw from all of these gifts and not depend upon the senior pastor for everything. The minds of the people must be renewed to accept and receive this order of ministry. They must be taught that this is God's order and that much of what the church has inherited was based on tradition more than revelation.

What we are seeing is a radical change in our whole concept of the church. Reformation always requires new teaching and restructuring of thought patterns. The people will not be able to handle such change as long as they are bound to old thought patterns. The leader must spend time teaching and training the people in new truth so that the entire church can transition into a new position.

Teaching helps release the apostolic. Teaching gives us a foundation to build upon. Whatever we do must be based upon the Word. Once people are convinced that what we are doing is scriptural, they can confidently embrace what we are building. Teaching helps us to make the adjustments and corrections needed to build accurately. Teaching exposes the false concepts and foundations that we have built upon in the past.

Teaching causes us to operate in truth. Truth sets us free. A new liberty will come in releasing the church to obey the will of God. Teaching also fortifies us against the attacks of darkness that will come for obeying the truth. Once people know that what they are walking in is truth, they will not compromise because of persecution. There can be no doubt in the minds of the people that the changes are scriptural. They must be convinced that this is of God.

The people must also see the benefits of change. People will not change if there is no benefit. Why go through all the difficulty of changing if there is no benefit? They need to see the blessing of changing into an apostolic church. They must see the greater blessings and power that will flow through their church as a result of change. Reformation always causes the blessings of God to be released in a greater way. Without reformation, the church becomes stagnant and eventually loses the full blessing of God. Through reformation, multitudes are blessed and released into their individual destinies. The church also begins to walk in corporate destiny and releases salvation and blessing to multitudes.

The diet of the church must change. They cannot continue to hear the same messages of the past and be expected to change. They must receive present truth and an understanding of current moves.

Transition is sometimes difficult because it requires humility and a willingness to make sacrifices. There will be a grace given by the Lord to make the change.

No man also having drunk old wine straightway desireth
new: for he saith, The old is better.

—LUKE 5:39

People must develop an appetite for new wine. Teaching helps
them develop a taste for the new wine. Once people hear about the
restoration of apostles and the function of apostolic ministry, they
will begin to develop a taste and appetite for it. The diet of the church
must change. They cannot continue to hear the same messages of the
past and be expected to change. They must receive present truth and
an understanding of current moves.

I also encourage leaders to recommend books for their leadership and members to read. There is no substitute for study. Make the
books available for the people. Allow them to read and study in their
time away from the services. You will not be able to do it all in a
Sunday morning service or a weekday Bible study. There is too much
to learn in a short period of time. Give the people the resources they
need to make the transition.

BRINGING *in* APOSTOLIC TEAMS

In addition to this, there is no substitute for bringing in an apostolic
team. Apostolic teams help upgrade the revelation of the local church.
Apostles and prophets help bring a revelation of the current moves of
God. Leaders often need outside help to move the people into a new
position. Revelation is a spirit, and those who have revelation can
impart it to the church. The people will see and understand things
through the teaching of anointed vessels. Those who have already
experienced this transition and are currently walking in these truths
can impart them to the church. What it took these vessels years to
move into, they will impart in a short period of time to those who
desire the impartation.

An *apostolic team* is a group of fivefold ministers, led by an apostle, that can come into a region or a church and build apostolically. The team comes to add to the church. They do not come to duplicate what the local leadership has already done. They help the church break through into new realms of spiritual power and revelation. We define *building apostolically* as "the grace and ability to root out, pull down, destroy, throw down, build, and plant" (Jer. 1:10). Apostles and apostolic teams have the authority to pull down and build up. They pull down the strongholds of darkness and build up the saints. When a team comes into a region, there will be breakthroughs and impartations released that will add momentum to the work.

There are conferences being held throughout the world emphasizing the restoration of the apostolic ministry. I am not referring to those who are just using the terminology, but those who gather with a genuine revelation, along with a desire to learn more and facilitate this move around the world. I commend the efforts of Dr. C. Peter and Doris Wagner for their desire to see this truth established in the church. Their conferences are helping and exposing many to true restoration of apostolic ministry. Gatherings of apostles and prophets help us to meet and relate to others who are of similar spirit and faith. This strengthens leaders and helps them to continue without feeling lonely or isolated. I believe that day is coming when you will see these kinds of gatherings in every nation. God is challenging leaders in every nation to make this transition, and He is making the way for them to meet and relate to others of like faith.

Chapter 10

ESTABLISHING *the* PROPHETIC MINISTRY—PROPHETS

Let the prophets speak two or three, and let the other judge. If any thing be revealed to another that sitteth by, let the first hold his peace. For ye may all prophesy one by one, that all may learn, and all may be comforted. And the spirits of the prophets are subject to the prophets.

—1 Corinthians 14:29–32

THE OTHER ELEMENT FOUND IN THE CHURCH AT ANTIOCH was the prophetic ministry. It was a combination of the teaching and prophetic ministries that helped birth the apostolic ministry. Local churches need to release and facilitate the prophetic ministry. The prophetic ministry should be a normal part of the ministry of the local church (1 Cor. 14:29–32).

Many apostolic leaders will be trained in a teaching or prophetic ministry before operating fully in an apostolic calling. There is a certain maturity needed to operate as an apostle. Barnabas and Paul were identified among the prophets and teachers before they were launched into their apostolic ministries. The calling to apostleship may be present, but the release comes after a season of preparation. Apostles need to be able to operate in strong prophetic and teaching ministries. If churches develop and strengthen these ministries, they will see a greater release of the apostolic.

This is not to imply that everyone who teaches or prophesies will become an apostle. *The calling of an apostle is sovereign and based upon the will of God.* There are people who are called to be teachers and prophets. They can have an apostolic spirit, but their primary calling will be as a prophet or a teacher.

Apostolic churches need to be places of strong teaching and strong prophetic ministry. There are many teaching centers that lack strong prophetic ministry. Many of them also lack a strong apostolic presence. If the dominant anointing of the church is teaching, the other gifts may be choked out. The teaching ministry is mentioned *third* in 1 Corinthians 12:28. To make it the dominating anointing of the local church is to be out of divine order. The problem becomes emphasizing teaching at the expense of the other ministry gifts. It is similar to the discussion we had previously concerning the pastor's anointing. This can happen when the senior pastor of the local church stays in a teaching mode and does not make the transition into an apostolic calling.

> The church is in dire need of prophetic ministry.
> There is no substitute for the prophetic.

Apostles teach as well as prophesy. There is more authority in the teaching of an apostle, because they will teach out of the strength of the apostolic office. Teaching must be in the church, and teachers must be released; but, teaching should not be the dominant anointing of the church. The apostolic spirit should be the foremost and primary spirit of the church. We should be first and foremost sent ones.

The same is true concerning the prophetic ministry. This ministry is mentioned as being *second* in the church. With the restoration of the teaching ministry in the seventies and eighties, we saw an emphasis on teaching. Many, however, did not add on the prophetic ministry when it was being restored in the eighties and early nineties. I have even heard preachers say, "We don't need prophecy; all we need is the Word!"

How can we read 1 Corinthians 12:28, which places prophetic ministry ahead of teachers, and undervalue the prophetic ministry? God has raised up many prophetic churches that activate and release believers to prophesy. The dominant anointing of the church, however, should not be prophetic. The prophetic ministry should be secondary to the apostolic ministry. This does not minimize the importance of the prophetic ministry. The church is in dire need of prophetic ministry. There is no substitute for the prophetic.

RAISING UP PROPHETS

Nevertheless, we are now seeing the restoration of apostolic ministry. This is not to say that men have not operated in this office before today. There have always been men who operated in this ministry throughout the history of the church. However, many churches have been robbed of this vital ministry through tradition and unbelief. With restoration, there will be a return of this ministry in its fullness and in abundance. God always restores what was lost, plus more. We are seeing many leaders rise up and accept their apostolic callings around the world. With the increase of knowledge and understanding concerning this subject, there are also a greater number of leaders embracing it.

Many of these leaders have come through the restoration of the teaching and prophetic moves. They are now being birthed through the present-day *apostolic* move. Their previous training in teaching and prophetic ministry has developed and matured them for this hour. The same is true concerning many churches. They have moved through the previous moves of restoration and are now poised for this present move. Churches need to receive the restoration of the prophetic ministry to be in a position to move apostolically.

Crusaders Church of Chicago was blessed in the 1990s to relate to Christian International and the ministry of Bishop Bill Hamon. God has used Christian International to help restore the prophetic ministry in a mighty way to the worldwide church. We began to send many of our leaders to Christian International conferences to be trained and activated in prophetic ministry. In addition to Christian International, we were blessed to relate to Pastors Buddy and Mary Crum and Life Center Church of Dunwoody, Georgia. Their activation workshops and prophetic team workshops helped train many of our current prophetic leaders. Hundreds of our members would drive and fly to these workshops to be activated and trained in prophetic ministry. As a result, we are currently activating and training hundreds of leaders around the world to minister prophetically.

We now have hundreds of people in our church who prophesy. We also have ordained prophets and prophetic teams that travel the nations. The release of the prophetic was a key step in the development of our church. One of the leaders of our prophetic ministry has been released to function as an apostle. He travels around the world with apostolic teams to help churches activate their leaders and members to prophesy. His development for apostolic ministry came through our prophetic ministry.

PROPHECY RELEASES *the* WILL *of* GOD *on the* EARTH

There are many things that will be birthed and released through prophecy. Prophetic utterances are instrumental in establishing the will of God upon the earth. There are many things that will not be released until someone declares it prophetically. In the beginning, God spoke and there was light. Light and revelation come from anointed utterances. The prophetic word releases, activates, initiates, exhorts, comforts, and confirms.

Prophetic utterances activate and release the plans and purposes of God. The prophetic word is creative. Prophecy not only informs us of what God is doing, but it actually triggers the move (Ps. 105:31, 34). Prophecy does more than confirm. Prophecy will also release. This is true concerning both personal prophecy and corporate prophecy.

Prophecy thrusts you into the purposes of God. It encourages you to move into the will of God. It releases faith to operate beyond what you are accustomed to.

Prophets carry a tremendous amount of authority. Their utterances break through the demonic opposition that is sent to hinder the plans and purposes of God. Churches that have strong prophetic utterance over individuals and regions will see a greater momentum and breakthrough in establishing what is being revealed by the Holy Spirit. The prophetic will help release the apostolic. The apostolic also releases the prophetic. These two ministries complement and stir one another.

For years we have heard prophetic words concerning the direction of our local church. Prophecies concerning our apostolic call were heard continually. We heard these things before we began to experience much of what we are walking in today. For years I received prophecies concerning an apostolic call. These words helped to encourage me to pursue and believe in the call. Apostolic leaders need the confirmation of proven prophetic ministries. This will encourage them and help to activate the gift inside.

Everything we are doing today was declared prophetically before we did it. Prophecy thrusts you into the purposes of God. It encourages you to move into the will of God. It releases faith to operate beyond what you are accustomed to. It helps to break the barriers and limitations we have accepted through tradition or lack of knowledge. Teaching on and releasing the prophetic ministry within the local church is integral. This is instrumental in helping a church move fully into an apostolic ministry.

PROPHETIC MINISTRY INCLUDES *the* SPIRIT *of* PROPHECY

When we speak of prophetic ministry, we are not limiting it to prophets. We are also including prophecy as one of the gifts of the Holy Spirit, and the spirit of prophecy that every believer has through the indwelling of the Holy Spirit. We make a distinction between the simple gift of prophecy and the ministry of the prophet. Every believer can prophesy (Acts 2:16–18). Prophecy is utterance that comes from being filled with the Spirit (Acts 19:6). We know that everyone is not a prophet (1 Cor. 12:29). Prophets prophesy with more authority and revelation because they speak from the strength and position of their office. The simple gift of prophecy, however, is speaking unto men for edification, exhortation, and comfort (1 Cor. 14:3).

Prophecy is a building gift. *To edify* means "to build." We get our word *edifice*, which means "a building or a structure," from this word. Prophecy is an integral part of building the church. When we build people, we build the church. Prophecy will strengthen believers, giving them the necessary strength to move into apostolic ministry. It strengthens and builds the spirits of the people. People with strong spirits will be able to transition and move into the fullness of what the Lord is releasing.

I cannot overemphasize the importance of prophecy. Churches should excel in it (1 Cor. 14:12). *To excel* means "to do extremely well." Our prophetic level should not be mediocre. We should not be average or sub-par in this area. People need to be activated and trained to flow in the spirit of prophecy. We need to take time to teach in this area and make room for its operation. It will not happen by accident. We must have a strategy to raise the level of the prophetic ministry in the local church.

Chapter 11

A NEW ORDER *for*
a NEW MOVE

But new wine must be put into new bottles; and both are preserved.

—Luke 5:38

And it came to pass in those days, that he went out into a mountain to pray, and continued all night in prayer to God. And when it was day, he called unto him his disciples: and of them he chose twelve, whom also he named apostles; Simon, (whom he also named Peter,) and Andrew his brother, James and John, Philip and Bartholomew, Matthew and Thomas, James the son of Alphaeus, and Simon called Zelotes, And Judas the brother of James, and Judas Iscariot, which also was the traitor.

—Luke 6:12–16

WHY DID JESUS CHOOSE TWELVE APOSTLES? WHY DIDN'T He choose twelve prophets or priests? Jesus ordained and released a new order of ministry. The ministry of an apostle is a New Testament ministry. Although Moses, Samuel, and David are Old Testament types of the apostle, they are identified as prophets.

Jesus was establishing a new order of ministry before the outpouring of the Holy Spirit on the Day of Pentecost. The Old Testament wineskin of Judaism with priests, prophets, judges, and kings could not handle the new wine of the Holy Spirit. The New Testament wineskin of the church, with the presence of apostles, is needed to contain the new wine.

Joel's prophecy emphasizes prophecy as an element of the last-day outpouring. The sons and daughters will prophesy. The servants and handmaidens will prophesy. The young men shall see visions and the old men dream dreams. This is a radical release of all people. It makes no difference whether you are male or female, young or old, rich or poor; all can prophesy and operate in a prophetic realm. In the Old Testament, only a select group was anointed to minister. The old wineskin of Judaism could not contain such a release of anointing. *The Holy Spirit releases all believers into ministry.*

Every reformation has brought about a release of all believers. The Protestant Reformation in the sixteenth century emphasized the priesthood of all believers. The Azusa revival of the twentieth century emphasized the Holy Spirit baptism and speaking in tongues for all believers. We have also learned that all believers can cast out devils, heal the sick, and do the works of Jesus (John 14:12). These things are no longer relegated to the clergy. Now we are seeing a release of all believers flowing prophetically and apostolically. This does not make all apostles and prophets, but all believers can operate in these dimensions.

God has raised up apostolic leaders to release believers throughout the history of the church. This is what the apostolic anointing is equipped to do. It takes an apostolic grace to be able to facilitate such releases. It has always been a radical concept to release the majority. Most religious leaders are afraid to do so. They are afraid they will lose control.

OLD WINESKIN *vs.* NEW WINESKIN

Apostles help create new wineskins. Old wineskins cannot handle this kind of expansion. Old wineskins are rigid and inflexible. Organizations and churches often become legalistic and dogmatic. It is their way or no way. When this happens, God raises up apostolic and prophetic leadership to bring a fresh word and help to create new wineskins. These anointings are more radical and progressive. They attract a new group of believers who are not held back and bound by a religious mind-set. The result is the formation of new wineskins.

> The spirit of revelation comes to open the eyes of believers to the truth. This truth is preached in spite of opposition. What was birthed in the heat of reformation becomes standard truth in the years to come.

Apostolic leaders will often be branded as troublemakers and heretics. Martin Luther was not the favorite preacher of many in his day. His preaching and teaching was radical. He put the Word of God into the hands of the common people. This broke the stranglehold of the privileged few. He upset the status quo. He dared to challenge the concept of clergy over laity.

The new wineskin comes into being when men rediscover truth. It has been there all the time but was hidden by the tradition of the church. The spirit of revelation comes to open the eyes of believers to the truth. This truth is preached in spite of opposition. What was birthed in the heat of reformation becomes standard truth in the years to come.

In order to transition successfully, a new wineskin must be developed. Leadership must concentrate on developing this new wineskin. The structure and format of the church must change. One cannot be afraid to change the structure of the church in order to create a new wineskin. The models of the past will not be sufficient to handle what God is doing today. We must receive the new blueprints that the Holy Spirit is giving us. Apostles are wise master builders (1 Cor. 3:10). They are spiritual architects. They build by revelation, not tradition.

Many of the models that leaders used to build are outmoded and outdated. We must upgrade our technologies and build according to the current patterns being released from heaven. The blueprints are here. We need to embrace them and believe they provide a structure that will cause a greater degree of blessing and glory to be released. You cannot put the new wine into old wineskins. The wineskins must change. There is no way to get around this truth.

There is room for all of the gifts to operate in an apostolic church. This ministry provides a framework large enough to house all God desires to do.

This is why apostles must be in place. The ministry of apostle is the new order of ministry for the outpouring of the new wine. Apostolic churches are new wineskins. The apostolic anointing is the only anointing capable of overseeing and releasing all believers into the fullness of what the Holy Spirit is releasing.

The PASTORAL MIND-SET

Most churches governed by a pastoral mentality have not been able to release the gifts of God fully. Many pastors are afraid to release prophecy, deliverance, and other supernatural ministries for fear of losing control. These things cannot be administrated and organized in the flesh. Many pastors think in terms of maintaining order and safety within the local church. The apostolic and prophetic gifts are

86

more radical and progressive. Apostles are pioneers and risk takers. They are not afraid to receive and release new things.

As long as our churches are governed by pastoral mind-sets, they will continue to see many gifts restricted and held back. There are many people with apostolic and prophetic gifts who are frustrated in churches because of leaders who are unable to release them. Many of these leaders have good hearts, but they lack the apostolic grace to facilitate what the Lord desires to do. There are also leaders with apostolic callings who cannot fully activate and release the people because they have been trained to think and operate pastorally. The pastoral mind-set has hindered many who have higher callings. Many leaders have been trained in Bible schools and seminaries to think pastorally and administratively. How many schools can one attend today that teach and train people to operate apostolically and prophetically?

The apostolic ministry has been set in the church to oversee and release all believers into their callings and destinies. The apostle's mind-set is conducive to accomplish this. The apostle should not think only in terms of maintaining but also in terms and areas of expanding. There is room for all of the gifts to operate in an apostolic church. This ministry provides a framework large enough to house all God desires to do. There is a capacity to contain the new wine without breakage and spillage. There is no limit to the number of ministries released when the leaders embrace and walk in an apostolic call.

The SIGNS of a TRUE APOSTLE

Not only did Jesus choose and ordain twelve apostles, but also He identified them. How does this apply to us today? The Lord is calling apostles forth around the world and identifying them. We are going to know who they are. He is calling them out of obscurity. They will no longer be hidden from the eyes of the church. We need to know the signs of a true apostle to test those who claim apostleship. Once they are identified, we can receive and benefit from their ministries.

Many of these leaders will be identified by their response to the truth. Their spirits will leap when they hear the message. There will be an excitement that comes. Their spirits will be charged, and they will have a hunger to know more. We are seeing this happen all over the world. The response has been overwhelming. It has been surprising to see how many leaders have been in preparation for this day.

Many of these leaders will also be identified prophetically. John the Baptist identified Jesus as the Lamb of God (John 1:29–34). Ananias identified Paul as a chosen vessel (Acts 9:10–16). Such leaders will receive the independent confirmation of proven prophetic ministries. I received a prophecy concerning apostolic ministry in 1989. At that time, I knew nothing about the ministry of the apostle. I had to pursue this ministry by faith. God has led me for these many years by His grace. Since then, I have received many confirming prophetic words.

These individuals can be identified by their works. Jesus pointed to His works to show He was a sent one (John 5:36). The work will speak for itself. There are many leaders who are presently doing apostolic work around the world. There are many who have not yet done the work, but the calling is there. They can draw up alongside of a proven apostolic ministry to be trained and matured.

The Twelve were identified as apostles before they ever planted a church. They were sent out by Jesus to preach, heal, cast out devils, and raise the dead. They would not have qualified for this ministry in the eyes of many today. They had no seminary training or divinity degrees. They were simply chosen, trained, and sent.

**A person who knows who he is becomes
a threat to the kingdom of darkness.**

Some would say, "It is not important to be called an apostle. Just do the work." I agree that it is better to have the work without the title than the title without the work. There are many who would claim apostleship without having the signs of a proven apostolic ministry. We are to test those who claim apostleship (Rev. 2:2). It is, however, important for people to know their gift and calling in order to be able to walk in it confidently and boldly. Jesus knew that He was sent. Paul identified himself as an apostle by the will of God. He even defended his apostleship.

When people do not know their identity, they will often miss their purpose. The devil tries to keep people from knowing who they are. He blinds the minds of many to keep them from their true identity. A person who knows who he is becomes a threat to the kingdom of darkness. Gideon did not know he was a mighty man of valor. Moses did not know he was the deliverer of Israel. They had to come into their identities to bring deliverance to Israel.

Identity is defined as "the condition of being oneself, and not another." What a powerful thought! When you know your identity, you can be yourself. You don't have to try to be what you are not. David could not wear Saul's armor. He was not comfortable trying to be what he was not. He used the weapons that were comfortable for him, and he killed Goliath. There are too many leaders trying to be what religion and tradition says they should be. They are trying to fit in a mold that they are not created for.

The apostolic leaders who are coming forth will not be identified by their association to a particular group or denomination. Paul was not a part of the Twelve. His call to apostleship was not based on their approval or knowledge. When he finally met James, Peter, and John, they recognized his apostolic call and extended to him the right hand of fellowship (Gal. 2:7–9). We cannot limit this ministry to our group or denomination. God chooses and calls whom He desires.

Those identified will take their place in the new order of ministry established by our Lord two thousand years ago. This ministry is one of the benefits of the New Testament. They have a better covenant based upon better promises. All shall know the Lord, from the least to the greatest (Heb. 8:8–12). This new covenant ministry, along with the other New Testament gifts, is for the perfecting of the saints. The saints will be matured to do the work of the ministry. The church will receive the full blessing of the covenant established by Jesus. The next chapters will deal with areas that must be strong in the local church if both the leaders and church expect to shift into an apostolic position. We have experienced these things in our local work in Chicago. The following are characteristics and ingredients of apostolic churches and apostolic people.

Chapter 12

PRAYER *and* DELIVERANCE

Pray ye therefore the Lord of the harvest, that he will send forth labourers into his harvest.

—MATTHEW 9:38

But we will give ourselves continually to prayer, and to the ministry of the word.

—ACTS 6:4

PRAYER RELEASES THE APOSTOLIC SPIRIT. PRAYER RELEASES sent ones. *Churches that want to transition into an apostolic position must have strong prayer and intercession.* The prayer base of the local church must be increased.

Prayer is also the power source of the apostolic. The apostles gave themselves continually to prayer. This is also true concerning apostolic churches. There will be a spirit of grace and supplication (Zech. 12:10). Apostles must be free from all of the normal administrative duties placed on most church leaders. They must be free to give themselves to prayer and the ministry of the Word. Many pastors work themselves to death with counseling and administrative duties. The people have come to expect the pastor to do everything. This is what he is paid to do, some may reason, but apostles must be released to cover a wider area of ministry. They must release themselves by releasing others. This is hard for some leaders to do. They have operated so long in a pastoral and administrative role that it will be hard for them to transition.

As we began to move into an apostolic position, intercession and prayer became a key to breakthrough into stronger realms of anointing. Jesus prayed all night before choosing the Twelve (Luke 6:12–13). All-night prayer is a key to releasing the apostolic spirit. The power released in prayer will give leaders and churches the strength they need to proceed. Corporate prayer was a characteristic of the early church (Acts 4:24). The whole church must be mobilized to prayer. Apostolic and prophetic leaders need to lead the congregation in strong praying.

Each time the Lord revealed to us new truth about the apostolic ministry, we would pray corporately concerning that truth. Whatever was preached, we would pray to be established. We prayed the prophecies that were spoken in our local church. We prayed for the grace to walk in what we were hearing. Prayer was an integral part of establishing the truth in our church.

We also bound the demon spirits in our region that were set on stopping what the Lord was saying. We prayed for angels to be released into our region to help us break through the resistance of the powers of darkness in our region. This must be done in prayer. We must war according to prophecy (1 Tim. 1:18).

Diversities of tongues is an important gift in this area (1 Cor. 12:28). Many prayer warriors will operate in diversities of tongues. There are great breakthroughs that will come through this gift. Utterances in other tongues will help us pray in a supernatural way, beyond the limitations of our understanding. We can pray beyond our limited understanding of what God is releasing and restoring.

Those who operate in the gift of diversities of tongues can release much through the various utterances of the Spirit.

Prayer neutralizes the powers of hell that would hinder believers from breaking through into new levels of revelation and grace.

The apostolic prayers of Paul are important to open the eyes of believers and cause them to know their calling. Paul prayed that the eyes of the church's understanding would be enlightened. He prayed for the believers to have the spirit of revelation (Eph. 1:17–18). He prayed that they would walk worthy of the Lord unto all pleasing, being fruitful in every good work, and increasing in the knowledge of God (Col. 1:10–11).

Apostolic churches must labor in prayer that the saints would stand perfect and complete in all the will of God (Col. 4:12). Prayer neutralizes the powers of hell that would hinder believers from breaking through into new levels of revelation and grace.

APOSTLES *and the* MINISTRY *of* DELIVERANCE

And when he had called unto him his twelve disciples, he gave them power against unclean spirits, to cast them out.
—MATTHEW 10:1

The first thing Jesus gave the Twelve before sending them forth was power over unclean spirits. Deliverance is a major part of the apostle's equipment to break through and establish the kingdom of God. The apostolic ministry is a ministry of liberty (2 Cor. 3:17). The people must be free to obey and walk in this ministry. This is why deliverance is a major key.

If demons are not exposed and cast out, they will hinder the purposes of God from being fulfilled. The more deliverance people receive, the freer they will be to walk in the Spirit and obey the Word of God. Casting out demons breaks the power of the enemy in a region and creates an environment of freedom. There will be a greater liberty in an apostolic church to believe and operate in power and anointing.

Because so many people need deliverance, we have no choice but to train and release multitudes of believers to cast out devils. This is the first sign that should follow a believer (Mark 16:17). Every believer needs to be mobilized to carry the apostolic burden of the local church. Apostolic churches are called to pull down strongholds in regions over which they have jurisdiction.

This is another reason why we must have an apostolic mentality prevailing in our churches. Deliverance is frightening to many leaders. They want to relegate it to a side room in the church instead of making it an integral part of the church. It is not a safe ministry. Dealing with demons is too unpleasant and risky for many leaders. They would rather spend hours counseling people who have demonic problems. Many want to substitute teaching for deliverance.

Apostles, however, are sent to destroy the works of the devil. Power and authority over demons is a sign of an apostolic ministry. Casting out devils is necessary to establish the kingdom of God (Matt. 12:18). Apostolic churches will manifest power and authority over the demons of a particular territory. This will give them the ability to penetrate and pioneer in that region.

Crusaders Church was exposed to the ministry of deliverance in 1985. At that time, we had no understanding of apostolic ministry. We did not know that what we were entering into was an apostolic function. Amid much controversy and misunderstanding, we were faithful to press into this ministry. It was laid in the foundation of our church, and it continues to be an integral part of the ministry.

Most of the members of Crusaders Church have received deliverance and have been trained to cast out devils. We taught for years in the area of deliverance, and we continue to do so. Books by Frank Hammond, Win Worley, Derek Prince, Don Basham, and other pioneers of the deliverance ministry helped to us understand the importance of deliverance. Books written recently by Bill Subritzky, Peter Horrobin, and Noel and Phyl Gibson are also powerful tools to instruct believers in the area of deliverance.

There is no substitute for the ministry of deliverance. The freedom that comes from casting out demons enables believers to rise to new levels of faith and obedience. It also opens the way for evangelism. The controlling powers of darkness are neutralized, and more people respond to the preaching of the gospel. It is a key to opening up entire regions to be evangelized. The heavens are opened, and the blessings of God are released.

Deliverance is necessary to attack and drive out religious spirits that have aborted and hindered much of what God desires to do. Spirits of witchcraft and generational spirits must also be challenged and driven out. Deliverance opens the way for holiness. Cleanliness and purity must be in place to keep the church from being diverted from its course.

There is no substitute for the ministry of deliverance. The freedom that comes from casting out demons enables believers to rise to new levels of faith and obedience.

Deliverance will strengthen the local church. Contending with demons and overcoming them will inspire faith and confidence. The level of discernment will also increase. Members will have their senses exercised to discern good and evil (Heb. 5:14). This will enable them to handle the strong meat of the Word. They will become adept in spiritual warfare and will be able to handle the pressure that comes with apostolic ministry. Apostolic ministry is a tough ministry that requires fortitude and perseverance. The experience gained in casting out demons is invaluable.

The APOSTLE *and* SPIRITUAL WARFARE

One of the functions of the apostolic ministry is warfare. The word translated "warfare" in 2 Corinthians 10:4 is the Greek word *strateia*, which means "apostolic career." The apostolic career is one of warfare. Deliverance helps the believers to learn warfare. God teaches our hands to war and our fingers to fight (Ps. 144:1). Apostolic churches are warring churches. They have the grace and anointing to pull down strongholds. There are many strongholds that will not be pulled down without an apostolic anointing.

Two of the outstanding characteristics of an apostolic ministry are power and authority (Matt. 10:1). There is an authority resident in the apostolic anointing to confront and pull down strongholds. These strongholds are the mind-sets that are contrary to the will of God. The rank of the apostle makes him a formidable combatant against the powers of darkness. Demons recognize and submit to this anointing.

God trains us through hand-to-hand combat with the enemy. Deliverance is often referred to as *ground-level warfare*. Apostolic churches become God's boot camp to train His army to invade and drive out the enemy. We have seen thousands of believers strengthened and trained through casting out demons. They must use their faith and gifts to deal with demons. They come to experientially know the victory of Christ over the enemy.

When believers deal with demons on a continual basis, they will mature in warfare. You will have a group of proven soldiers who will be able to contend with the powers of darkness on a higher level. The church can then be successful in *strategic-level warfare*.

This is dealing with territorial spirits that control a region or a territory. Breakthroughs in these territories are contingent upon the binding of these powers. Once these powers are bound, there will be a new liberty and openness to the gospel in that region.

Chapter 13

DEVELOPING TEAMS

And he ordained twelve, that they should be with him, and that he might send them forth to preach.

—MARK 3:14

JESUS ORDAINED THE TWELVE TO BE A PART OF HIS TEAM. AS members of His team, they could then be sent forth. As leaders develop teams, they will be able to send the team members forth. Apostolic leaders ordain and release. This is the pattern of ministry given by our Lord. Jesus is the Apostle of our profession. He is the perfect Apostle. As an apostle, He released other apostles. We will see apostles who ordain and release other apostles.

If a leader is to make a successful transition from a pastoral into an apostolic role, he must develop a team of leaders that will help carry the burden of ministry. Without a strong team, the burden of ministry in the local work will fall directly upon him. The development of the team will help release the leader into an apostolic role. It will free him to move out into a greater ministry to the larger body of Christ. It is crucial to release pastors to tend to the flock. It is also important to develop a team of governmental leaders who continue to give direction and oversight to the work.

In Crusaders Church, we have seen a team of apostles, prophets, and teachers come together to guard and direct the work. The apostolic leaders are able to take teams around the world to impact nations. The prophets are released to help give direction and insight into what the Lord is directing us to do. The teachers are released to train new members and believers as well as to provide a strong Word foundation for members of the church. These governmental anointings work together as a team. The work has grown too large for one man and a few assistants to handle.

We have also developed apostolic teams (to send to nations), prophetic teams (to minister prophetically to large numbers of people), praise and worship teams, deliverance and healing teams, prayer teams, evangelistic teams, and dance teams. Believers are encouraged to be a part of a ministry team and to minister using their gifts to those in need.

APOSTOLIC MINISTRY IS TEAM MINISTRY

The traditional concept of having one pastor and some associates to pastor the flock is being challenged. Jesus gathered a team around Him and trained them for three and one-half years. He also sent out the Seventy in teams of two (Luke 10:1). The Antioch church released apostolic teams to plant churches and travel throughout the known world. We are now developing and establishing presbyteries that will be able to govern the local church. These presbyteries will consist of apostles, prophets, and teachers, which are the governing gifts of the church (1 Cor. 12:28). They will serve as a team that gives direction and covering for the local church.

The presbytery is able to prophesy and impart (1 Tim. 4:14). They have an apostolic mentality because they have apostolic leadership within the presbytery. The order and ranking of ministry is respected within the presbytery. From the presbytery, leaders can be released for ministry outside the local church, just as at the church in Antioch. The church becomes an apostolic resource center because of developed leaders who can be released at the leading of the Holy Spirit.

> When the Antioch church becomes our
> model church, the church migrates from
> a pastoral position to an apostolic one
> without losing the pastoral dimension.

The *presbytery* is the team that oversees and gives direction to the local church. This keeps the church strong and makes it a powerful witness in the community. *Apostolic teams* are groups that are sent out to affect regions beyond the local area. Some leaders can function in both. When at home, the leaders can be part of the presbytery. When going out, they can be part of an apostolic team. Some will be set primarily in the presbytery. Some will spend more time going out as part of an apostolic team.

This concept of ministry needs to be taught to the church. Believers must come into agreement with it and make the necessary changes to accommodate it. The Antioch church becomes our model church. When this happens, the church begins to migrate from a pastoral position to an apostolic one without losing the pastoral dimension. The members will still be cared for because of the release of pastors. The church will move beyond being a parish and have a greater impact in different regions and territories. This includes planting churches and building apostolically in the places where teams are sent.

A TEAM IS STRONGER THAN ONE MAN

A team of apostles, prophets, and teachers carries tremendous authority in the spirit realm. The powers of hell must recognize the authority of these teams and submit. The church needs to be able to release apostolic teams, prophetic teams, evangelistic teams, and deliverance teams to other churches and regions. This will give an apostle a greater ability to impact and influence a wider territory than he can influence by himself.

Many churches are led by a charismatic leader who may have a pastoral staff to assist him. The ministry revolves around this one leader. This is a pastoral mentality that must be changed to release other apostles, prophets, and teachers, as well as pastors and evangelists. As a leader shifts into an apostolic role, he must develop and release teams of strong ministers. He cannot be intimidated by strong gifts and anointings. The Lord will send many strong gifts to an apostle because of the grace upon this ministry to activate, train, and release gifts. They are not sent to support his ministry only, but to be instrumental in fulfilling the apostolic vision given to the church. Some will be sent out as apostles to plant churches and duplicate in other places what they have seen at the home base. Teams will be released to go to nations to extend the kingdom of God.

> **Presbyteries to apostolic teams are keys to churches being able to reach out to nations. Presbyteries provide a pool of proven ministries. From this pool, the Holy Spirit can draw and send out.**

The Antioch church illustrates the team concept. The church at Jerusalem sent Barnabas to help with the work (Acts 11:22). Barnabas departed to Tarsus to recruit Paul to come and help with the work. Barnabas and Paul assembled themselves at Antioch to teach for a year (Acts 11:25–26). They labored together as a team at Antioch. They were later sent out as a team from Antioch (Acts 13:1–4).

First Thessalonians 2 gives us revelation concerning the apostolic team. The team exhorts, teaches, preaches, comforts, charges, and imparts. A team consists of leaders with different anointings whose gifts complement each other. They work together, and each member lends his/her strength to the whole. The devil hates and fears the work of the team. The team can break through where one person cannot.

Churches that develop presbyteries and apostolic teams will take on the burden for entire nations and regions. They will have the capacity to touch these regions because they will have teams available to be released. Their governmental structure enables them to reach out without the home base falling apart. People are their greatest resources and apostolic grace enables them to do more than the average church. They become models that can be reproduced and multiplied in other places.

Presbyteries to apostolic teams are keys to churches being able to reach out to nations. Presbyteries provide a pool of proven ministries. From this pool, the Holy Spirit can draw and send out. The apostolic team is God's end-time strategy to affect nations. The line (measure) of the church must extend to the uttermost parts of the earth. Our ability to reach out and touch multitudes in a personal way is proportionate to the development and release of apostolic teams.

The APOSTOLIC WILL CHANGE the LIFESTYLE of the CHURCH

The results of shifting from a pastoral mode to an apostolic mode will be numerous. The very nature of the church will change. This includes its emphasis and lifestyle. The members will begin to adopt an apostolic lifestyle that will change the way they think, act, and live. They will develop a team mentality. Every area of the church will be affected. This includes the preaching, teaching, prayer, worship, finances, vision, and outreach.

The messages from the pulpit will change. The content of the messages will be deeper and will affect those who hear them in a deeper way. More revelation will come forth that will cause the believers to have an understanding of the mysteries of God. The messages will emphasize the corporate destiny of the church. Revelation will change the church and cause the believers to live a lifestyle that is opposed to the individualistic way of thinking that most people live by.

The strategies of the church will change. Apostolic strategies will come forth, enabling the church to execute the plans and purposes of God. This strategy will include teams. This is a higher way of thinking that is conducive to carrying out the commissions given to the church. New spiritual technologies will be released that will give the church the ability to do what could not be done previously.

The people will experience a greater degree of glory and liberty. When the dominant anointing is apostolic, the people will come into contact with a higher frequency and will become accustomed to it. They will be able to operate in higher levels of anointing, and they will live and minister in higher levels of glory.

Apostles will challenge and demand performance from the saints. Pastors have been guilty of doing the work for the people, whereas apostles demand that the people rise to a new level of maturity. The dependency upon the pastor is broken. The saints are expected to grow and perform on a higher level. The apostolic ministry raises the standard and expects more. It is not a caretaker, babysitting ministry.

Apostles will mobilize large groups of people for ministry. Jesus released the Twelve, and then He released the Seventy. They were able to duplicate His ministry of preaching, healing, and deliverance throughout Israel. He then released the disciples to go into all the world and teach all nations. The apostolic ministry is one of duplication and multiplication.

The church should not have to depend upon mission boards and parachurch ministries to fulfill the Great Commission. The church is responsible for destroying the gates of hell.

Teams make it possible for more people to exercise their gifts. When the responsibilities of ministry are shared, more people get involved. As more people come into the kingdom, we will have no choice but to develop and release teams. The needs of humanity are too great. If we are believing for a harvest, we must prepare to meet their needs. God has released an abundance of gifts to meet the needs of the lost. We are living in a day of abundance of grace. The apostolic ministry is a ministry of great grace (Acts 4:33).

As the church's vision expands, and it will, once a shift is made into the apostolic, the necessity to raise up teams will become obvious. God will put the multitudes in our hearts.

People respond to the supernatural. Everywhere Jesus went, He was overwhelmed by the crowds. He had to train and release a team to minister to the multitudes. When we started our deliverance ministry, we were overwhelmed by the number of people who came for ministry. We quickly had to train hundreds of deliverance workers to minister to those needing help. The same was true concerning prophetic ministry. The response to the prophetic was overwhelming. We had to train hundreds of people to be able to minister the Word of the Lord to those who came for ministry.

As the church's vision expands, and it will, once a shift is made into the apostolic, the necessity to raise up teams will become obvious. God will put the multitudes in our hearts. We will carry the burden of helping the multitudes. We will develop the means to touch them. People are our greatest resources. There is no substitute for anointed people. They are the tools to get the job done.

Chapter 14

RELEASING
APOSTOLIC TEAMS

Now there were in the church that was at Antioch certain prophets and teachers; as Barnabas, and Simeon that was called Niger, and Lucius of Cyrene, and Manaen, which had been brought up with Herod the tetrarch, and Saul. As they ministered to the Lord, and fasted, the Holy Ghost said, Separate me Barnabas and Saul for the work whereunto I have called them. And when they had fasted and prayed, and laid their hands on them, they sent them away.

—ACTS 13:1–3

WE DEFINE AN ANTIOCH CHURCH AS "AN APOSTOLIC, governmental church that impacts regions and territories." These churches are spiritual hubs. They are strategic churches raised up by God to initiate apostolic endeavors across the earth. In his book *The Normal Christian Church Life*, Watchman Nee said:

The church in Antioch is the model church shown us in God's Word because it was the first to come into being after the founding of the churches connected with the Jews and the Gentiles. In Acts chapter two we see the church in connection with the Jews established in Jerusalem, and in chapter ten we see the church in connection with the Gentiles established in the house of Cornelius. It was just after the establishment of these churches that the church in Antioch from the very outset stood on absolutely clear church ground. It is of no little significance that the disciples were first called Christians in Antioch (Acts 11:26). It was there that the peculiar characteristics of the Christian and the Christian church were first clearly manifested, for this reason it may be regarded as the pattern church for this dispensation.

It is in this framework that an atmosphere for the development and release of apostolic teams is provided. Apostolic teams consist of apostles with other fivefold ministry giftings who are able to go into a region and build apostolically. Apostles will lead the team and draw from the other anointings (especially from prophets) to break through in churches and territories to which they have been sent. The team preaches, teaches, prophesies, and operates in the gifts of the Holy Spirit. They will also minister deliverance and healing. The apostolic team is a part of God's strategy to release the plan and purposes of God throughout the earth.

The apostolic team imparts a fresh Spirit measure into the churches and regions they visit. They release new revelation and present truth to the believers. The team ignites new moves of the Holy Spirit and brings upgrades in spiritual technologies. One of God's end-time strategies is the release of apostolic teams. (The apostolic team does not come to duplicate what the local leadership has already produced, but rather to release a new Spirit measure into the church.)

There is a Macedonian call throughout the earth for the apostolic team (Acts 16:13). Many churches and regions need the help of these teams. Local churches and regions would do well to bring in an apostolic team. The apostolic team will bring blessing, refreshing, revelation, and impartation.

The apostolic team is a way of connecting governing apostolic churches to different churches, regions, and nations. The spiritual deposit and resources that exist in the apostolic church can be distributed throughout the nations through apostolic teams. The local church can have more than one apostolic team. This can be done by recognizing other apostolic leaders within the church (or network) and releasing them to head teams that are sent out. In this way, the local church can affect many regions and nations.

The apostolic team is important because no apostle can do all the work required of apostolic ministry alone. Jonathan David states, "To meet the intensity of his own burden to build strong local churches an apostle knows that raising up an apostolic team of builders alongside him is not only necessary but vital to have ministry success."

The apostolic team must be able to bring new revelation and teaching of the Word. They must upgrade churches and regions with new insights from heaven.

The apostle attracts and releases other fivefold ministers. This is one of the most important functions of apostolic ministry. Teams can break through where individuals cannot. Apostles and prophets working together make a formidable team in the Spirit.

The First Team

The first team released from Antioch consisted of Barnabas and Paul. They also took with them John Mark (Acts 13:5). This group gives us a picture of what is needed within a team. We know that

both Barnabas and Paul flowed prophetically because they are identified as prophets in Acts 13:1. Barnabas's name means "the son of
consolation" (Acts 4:36). Barnabas was an encourager. He came to
Antioch and exhorted the new church to cleave unto the Lord (Acts
11:22–23). This is important because one of the main functions of the
apostolic team is to encourage and comfort. Barnabas-type apostles
and prophets are needed on the apostolic team.

Paul was a man well versed in the Scriptures. He was an apostle
of revelation. He was focused and entirely sold out concerning his
commission. He was able to teach and preach because of his diligent
study of the Word. This is important because the apostolic team must
be able to bring new revelation and teaching of the Word. They must
upgrade churches and regions with new insights from heaven. We
need Paul-type apostles and prophets on the team that are skillful in
the Word and able to impart truth to believers.

John Mark was a young man who turned back on the first
journey. There is no detail given concerning why he returned before
the first journey was complete. We can only speculate that he was not
willing or able at that time to handle the rigors of apostolic ministry.
This eventually caused a separation between Barnabas and Paul.
Barnabas wanted to take him on the second trip, but Paul refused.
Evidently, Barnabas's encouraging nature would not let him give up
on John Mark (Acts 15:37–41). Mark consequently matured, because
Paul later called for him while in prison (2 Tim. 4:11).

Mark represents an understudy apostle. It is good to have those
on the team who are being trained and mentored. We must not
neglect young people who have callings and destinies that need to
be released. We now have the Gospel of Mark because of Barnabas's
encouragement.

The SECOND TEAM

The second team consisted of Paul and Silas. We have already mentioned Paul's characteristics. Silas is called a prophet in Acts 15:32. He was an exhorter and helped confirm the churches. He is referred to as one of the "chief men among the brethren" (Acts 15:22). He is referred to as an apostle (1 Thess. 1:1; 2:6–7). He was not a novice but was recognized as a leader in the Jerusalem church. He is a prophetic apostle who labored on the apostolic team to confirm and strengthen the churches.

Members of the apostolic team should not use the
team as a means of promoting their own ministries.
People who are self-seeking and have worldly
ambition should not be part of an apostolic team.

Timothy also became a part of this team. He is referred to as a faithful son in the ministry by Paul. He was taught the Scriptures from an early age (2 Tim. 3:15). He is another example of an understudy apostle. Paul told him to let no man despise his youth (1 Tim. 4:12). This shows us the importance of having young people on the apostolic team.

Timothy was not self-seeking (Phil. 2:19–21). Members of the apostolic team should not use the team as a means of promoting their own ministries. People who are self-seeking and have worldly ambition should not be part of an apostolic team.

OTHER TEAM MEMBERS

Other team members include Titus, Epaphroditus, Sopater, Aristarchus, Secundus, Gaius, Tychicus, and Trophimus (2 Cor. 12:18; Phil. 2:25; Acts 20:4). Titus was left in Crete to ordain elders and set things in order (Titus 1:5). These are both apostolic functions.

Titus was evidently a man who could operate in biblical order and authority. He was able to handle responsibility. Team members must be responsible and trustworthy.

Epaphroditus was a hard worker, a fighter, and one who ministered to Paul's wants (Phil. 2:25). He had a servant's heart. Apostolic team members should have servant's hearts. They should also have a soldier's mentality. They must be able to endure hardship.

One of the signs of a true apostle is the ability to gather other ministry gifts for training, activation, and release. This was a characteristic of Paul's ministry. The following scriptures give us a picture of the many people associated with his team.

> So he sent into Macedonia two of them that ministered unto him, Timotheus and Erastus; but he himself stayed in Asia for a season....And the whole city was filled with confusion: and having caught Gaius and Aristarchus, men of Macedonia, Paul's companions in travel, they rushed with one accord into the theatre.
>
> —ACTS 19:22, 29

> Timotheus my workfellow, and Lucius, and Jason, and Sosipater, my kinsmen, salute you. I Tertius, who wrote this epistle, salute you in the Lord. Gaius mine host, and of the whole church, saluteth you. Erastus the chamberlain of the city saluteth you, and Quartus a brother.
>
> —ROMANS 16:21–23

Roger Sapp, author of *The Last Apostles on Earth*, states, "Whenever you find this ministry, you should find individuals like Timothy and others whom God is discipling in ministry by means of the apostle. The apostle will always have individuals God has given him to train. He will have young prophets, teachers, evangelists, and pastors to encourage and prepare for greater ministry than his own. God will call some of them into apostolic ministry as well."

The apostolic team is a practical way of training ministers through hands-on ministry. The apostle has a grace to train and release ministry teams quickly.

In addition to those being trained, mature elders should be released from the presbytery to be a part of the team. This will make room for others in the local church to rise up and fill the vacancies. The result will be the continual development of strong ministry gifts within the local church and a continual release of qualified leaders to be a part of apostolic teams. This will break stagnation in the local church that results when there is no release of apostolic teams.

> The apostolic team confirms and exhorts
> believers in the local churches, especially in
> places where the church is persecuted.

The following are principles gleaned from the Word of God concerning apostolic teams. Many of them are taken from Paul's first letter to the Thessalonians.

1. The mission of the apostolic team

The apostolic team brings salvation to the ends of the earth.

> For so hath the Lord commanded us, saying, I have set thee to be a light of the Gentiles, that thou shouldest be for salvation unto the ends of the earth.
>
> —ACTS 13:47

Jonathan David, author of *Apostolic Strategies Affecting Nations*, calls the apostolic team "God's strategic plan to reach the nations." Acts 13:47 is a quote from Isaiah 49:6. Paul saw the apostolic ministry as one that brings salvation to the ends of the earth. Antioch churches will release apostolic teams to the nations. They will bring deliverance to many regions beyond the local church. The apostolic team brings light and revelation to regions of spiritual darkness and ignorance. The apostolic team is sent by the command of God. This means they are sent with the authority of heaven. Their authority is recognized by the spirit realm in the regions where they are sent.

2. The need for the apostolic team

The apostolic team confirms and exhorts believers in the local churches, especially in places where the church is persecuted.

> And when they had preached the gospel to that city, and had taught many, they returned again to Lystra, and to Iconium, and Antioch, Confirming the souls of the disciples, and exhorting them to continue in the faith, and that we must through much tribulation enter into the kingdom of God.
>
> —ACTS 14:21–22

Apostolic teams are especially needed in nations where the church suffers persecution. They will confirm these churches and exhort them. *To confirm* means "to strengthen." It is important to strengthen churches that have suffered, that they may be able to continue their witness. God will use Antioch churches to strengthen other churches that live in difficult regions of the world. The visit of the apostolic team will help believers continue in the faith.

3. The authority of the apostolic team

The apostolic team can ordain elders in the churches they plant and establish.

> And when they had ordained them elders in every church, and had prayed with fasting, they commended them to the Lord, on whom they believed.
>
> —ACTS 14:23

This is the beginning of the reproduction of presbyteries and apostolic teams. Once a new presbytery has been established in a region, they are responsible to seek the Lord and eventually release apostolic teams. God is a God of multiplication and increase. These are proven strategies to impact regions and fulfill the Great Commission.

4. The decrees of the apostolic team

The apostolic team delivers apostolic decrees and keeps the local churches operating in the liberty of the Spirit.

> And as they went through the cities, they delivered them the decrees for to keep, that were ordained of the apostles and elders which were at Jerusalem.
>
> —ACTS 16:4

The first doctrinal controversy in the church was concerning the Law. Some Jewish believers were teaching that the Gentiles had to be circumcised and keep the Law of Moses. The church convened in Jerusalem to resolve the issue. They issued a decree to the Gentile churches that freed them from the requirement of circumcision and the Law. A team was sent to deliver the decree.

The issue was liberty. Satan always attempts to stop the liberty of the local churches. Apostolic teams help the local churches maintain the liberty of the Holy Spirit. They break off man-made restrictions and rules that hinder the church. Apostolic ministry releases liberty (2 Cor. 3:17).

5. The strength of the apostolic team

The apostolic team helps the local churches become established in the faith and helps the local churches to grow.

> And so were the churches established in the faith, and increased in number daily.
>
> —ACTS 16:5

The apostolic team helps establish the believers of the local church. *To establish* means "to make secure, stable, or permanent." The church must be established in order to be strong.

Once churches are established they are put in a position for growth. Apostolic ministry is necessary to the health and vitality of the church. The apostolic team releases an anointing for church growth. Churches become stronger and healthier after a visit from the apostolic team.

6. The leading of the apostolic team

The apostolic team must be led by the Holy Spirit.

> Now when they had gone throughout Phrygia and the region of Galatia, and were forbidden of the Holy Ghost to preach the word in Asia.
>
> —ACTS 16:6

There may be places where the team is forbidden to go. Jesus governs the team through the Holy Spirit. He is the One directing and leading the team. This is what makes the team successful. The team depends upon the leading of the Holy Spirit.

There is a Macedonian call being sent through the earth for apostolic teams to come and help.

Apostolic teams must not be presumptuous. They cannot operate in fleshly wisdom but are entirely dependent upon the Holy Spirit. New territories must be approached only by the Lord's direction. To go any other way is to invite disaster or failure.

7. The call for the apostolic team

The apostolic team responds to the call of regions that need help.

> And a vision appeared to Paul in the night; There stood a man of Macedonia, and prayed him, saying, Come over into Macedonia, and help us. And after he had seen the vision, immediately we endeavoured to go into Macedonia, assuredly gathering that the Lord had called us for to preach the gospel unto them.
>
> —Acts 16:9–10

Antioch churches will respond to the Macedonian call of churches in need of help. The apostolic team is anointed by God to help. It is the nature and desire of the apostolic team to help build up churches. There is a Macedonian call being sent through the earth for apostolic teams to come and help.

As we build apostolic teams, we will be in a position to respond to this call for help.

8. The power of the apostolic team

The apostolic team breaks the power of python.

> And it came to pass, as we went to prayer, a certain damsel possessed with a spirit of divination met us, which brought her masters much gain by soothsaying: The same followed Paul and us, and cried, saying, These men are the servants of the most high God, which shew unto us the way of salvation. And this did she many days. But Paul, being grieved, turned and said to the spirit, I command thee in the name of Jesus Christ to come out of her. And he came out the same hour.
>
> —Acts 16:16–18

This is the only detailed apostolic deliverance given in the Bible. In this passage, the spirit of divination is the spirit of python. A python is a constrictor. This spirit will slowly choke the life out of the church. Pythons kill their victims by squeezing the breath out of

115

them. When python's power is broken, there will be a greater liberty in the church. The church will be able to breathe again.

The apostolic team will help destroy the spirit of witchcraft. Churches that are in regions where there is strong witchcraft will benefit from the visit of the apostolic team. Believers in the local churches will receive deliverance from witchcraft spirits and generational curses. This will release them to flow in the gifts and operations of the Holy Spirit.

9. The entrance of the apostolic team

The apostolic team has an entrance provided by the Lord.

> For yourselves, brethren, know our entrance in unto you, that it was not in vain.
>
> —1 THESSALONIANS 2:1

God opens the door for the apostolic team. We should pray for great and effectual doors to be opened (1 Cor. 16:9). God will set before us open doors that no man can shut (Rev. 3:8). When the door is opened and the people respond, the entrance is not in vain. The apostolic team should expect great results.

10. The boldness of the apostolic team

The apostolic team ministers in boldness.

> But even after that we had suffered before, and were shamefully entreated, as ye know, at Philippi, we were bold in our God to speak unto you the gospel of God with much contention.
>
> —1 THESSALONIANS 2:2

Boldness is a characteristic of the apostolic ministry. Team members need to operate in boldness and not be intimidated by opposition or persecution. Paul and his team were bold in Thessalonica in spite of being jailed previously in Philippi. The attacks of darkness should not stop the apostolic team.

False apostles and prophets operate in deceit, especially in the area of finances. True apostles and prophets are driven by a commission, not financial gain.

---

11. The purity of the apostolic team

The apostolic team has pure motives.

> For our exhortation was not of deceit, nor of uncleanness, nor in guile.
>
> —1 THESSALONIANS 2:3

The apostolic team does not operate in deceit or deception. People on the apostolic team speak the truth with pure hearts. They do not come to mislead. They must have pure motives. False apostles and prophets operate in deceit, especially in the area of finances. True apostles and prophets are driven by a commission, not financial gain. They have no ulterior motives.

12. The trust of the apostolic team

The apostolic team's desire is to please God.

> But as we were allowed of God to be put in trust with the gospel, even so we speak; not as pleasing men, but God, which trieth our hearts.
>
> —1 THESSALONIANS 2:4

The apostolic team has been entrusted with a message. The team cannot violate this trust. They must be faithful to preach and release the revelation committed to them by God. This is an awesome responsibility, and the team will one day be judged based on this trust.

13. The motive of the apostolic team

Pleasing God is the motivation of the apostolic team. The team does not have a man-pleasing spirit. Many religious groups have a desire to please men. This is not the case with the apostolic team. Sometimes their message may be controversial or offensive in the eyes of men.

The apostolic team does not minister for financial gain.

> For neither at any time used we flattering words, as ye know, nor a cloke of covetousness; God is witness.
>
> —1 Thessalonians 2:5

The ministry is not a cloak of covetousness for the apostolic team. They do not preach messages for financial gain. Covetous people should not be a part of an apostolic team. Financial gain is not the motive of the team. They go because they are sent. Sent ones are driven by a commission, not money.

14. The humility of the apostolic team

The apostolic team should never be a burden to the local church.

> Nor of men sought we glory, neither of you, nor yet of others, when we might have been burdensome, as the apostles of Christ.
>
> —1 Thessalonians 2:6

The apostolic team must never become a financial burden to the local churches. This does not mean that the local churches should not bless the team financially. There are, however, places where the apostolic team will go that cannot afford to bring an entire team. This is especially true of poor regions.

The members of an apostolic team can support themselves if necessary (1 Thess. 2:9).

15. The gentleness of the apostolic team

The apostolic team ministers in gentleness.

> But we were gentle among you, even as a nurse cherisheth her children.
>
> —1 Thessalonians 2:7

The team will not be "hard" on the church. They minister with care and compassion. They do not come to beat the sheep but to bless the sheep. False apostles will smite you on the face, but the team ministers by the meekness and gentleness of Christ (2 Cor. 11:20; 10:1). Sent ones are not harsh and dictatorial.

The apostolic team will impart their very lives into the believers of the local churches. They pour out their hearts to the people.

---

16. The impartation of the apostolic team

The apostolic team imparts their very life into the local church.

> So being affectionately desirous of you, we were willing to have imparted unto you, not the gospel of God only, but also our own souls, because ye were dear unto us.
>
> —1 Thessalonians 2:8

Impartation is one of the main goals of the apostolic team. The apostolic team will impart their very lives into the believers of the local churches. They pour out their hearts to the people. They give whatever they have willingly to the local churches. This is not just preaching or teaching but impartation. This is what makes apostolic team ministry so powerful. The team lays down their lives for the local church.

17. The sacrifice of the apostolic team

The apostolic team will be willing to make financial sacrifices if necessary.

> For ye remember, brethren, our labour and travail: for labouring night and day, because we would not be chargeable unto any of you, we preached unto you the gospel of God.
> —1 Thessalonians 2:9

Members of the apostolic team should be willing to make financial sacrifices if necessary to touch the nations. Some will be able to finance certain trips. God will honor these sacrifices. This will also prove that the team is not in ministry for financial gain.

18. The conduct of the apostolic team

The apostolic team must behave "holily and justly and unblameably." They set an example for the local church to follow.

> Ye are witnesses, and God also, how holily and justly and unblameably we behaved ourselves among you that believe.
> —1 Thessalonians 2:10

> For yourselves know how ye ought to follow us: for we behaved not ourselves disorderly among you.
> —2 Thessalonians 3:7

The apostolic team must conduct itself in the highest standard. No one on the team must give the devil a chance to bring reproach. A reproach on the team is also a reproach to the sending church. Nothing must be said or done that is sinful or even appears to be evil. The team must be a model for the church they minister in. There must be no strife or division between team members.

19. The heart of the apostolic team

The apostolic team exhorts, comforts, and charges the local church.

> For our exhortation was not of deceit, nor of uncleanness, nor in guile. As ye know how we exhorted and comforted and charged every one of you, as a father does his children.
> —1 Thessalonians 2:3, 11

The apostolic team will exhort, comfort, and charge the local church. *To exhort* means "to call near." The team calls the church near to God. The church will experience a closer relationship to the Lord. The team does not come to draw people to themselves but to God.

The apostolic team must conduct itself in the highest standard. No one on the team must give the devil a chance to bring reproach. A reproach on the team is also a reproach to the sending church.

The apostolic team exhorts the church to prayer, holiness, love, worship, praise, and giving. *To comfort* means "to encourage or console." This is important, especially to churches that have had trouble.

To charge means "to scourge." The apostolic team is able to bring correction. This is based on the relationship that has formed between the two, likened to that of a father and his children. Correction must come out of relationship. There exists a bond of genuine love between the apostolic team and the local churches.

20. The standard of the apostolic team

The apostolic team influences the local church to walk worthy of God.

> That ye would walk worthy of God, who hath called you
> unto his kingdom and glory.
>
> —1 THESSALONIANS 2:12

The ministry of the apostolic team will cause the church to walk worthy of God. They lift the standard of holiness and righteousness for the church. They encourage the saints to walk in love, unity, and sanctification that is well pleasing to God. The team's goal is to cause the saints to experience kingdom living. The kingdom of God has higher standards than the world.

21. The results of the apostolic team

The word of the apostolic team will work effectually in the believers.

> For this cause also thank we God without ceasing, because,
> when ye received the word of God which ye heard of us,
> ye received it not as the word of men, but as it is in truth,
> the word of God, which effectually worketh also in you that
> believe.
>
> —1 THESSALONIANS 2:13

The Word deposited into the church by the apostolic team will work effectually in the believers. The Word will continue to work even after the team has departed. The Amplified Version of 1 Thessalonians 2:13 says, "... exercising its superhuman power in those who adhere to and trust in and rely on it." The apostolic team can expect the Word deposited to work supernaturally in the church. Apostolic ministry has always been God's pattern for the church, and it brings supernatural results.

22. The model of the apostolic team

The apostolic team releases a model for the churches to follow.

> For ye, brethren, became followers of the churches of God which in Judaea are in Christ Jesus: for ye also have suffered like things of your own countrymen, even as they have of the Jews.
>
> —1 Thessalonians 2:14

The apostolic team is able to duplicate the model from which they are sent. Antioch churches will release a model for apostolic churches to be raised up in different nations. The team comes with blueprints that the churches can build with. The Knox translation of 1 Thessalonians 2:14 says, "You took for your model, brethren, the churches of God which are assembled in Judaea in the name of Jesus Christ."

23. The return of the apostolic team

The apostolic team should desire to return.

> But we, brethren, being taken from you for a short time in presence, not in heart, endeavoured the more abundantly to see your face with great desire.
>
> —1 Thessalonians 2:17

> For God is my record, how greatly I long after you all in the bowels of Jesus Christ.
>
> —Philippians 1:8

Although the team leaves physically, their heart remains with the local church. They will desire to return and be a blessing again. This is because there is a genuine bond in the spirit between the team and the local church.

24. The opposition to the apostolic team

Satan will often attempt to prevent the apostolic team from returning.

> Wherefore we would have come unto you, even I Paul, once and again; but Satan hindered us.
>
> —1 Thessalonians 2:18

Satan hates and fears the visit of the apostolic team. He will do everything in his power to prevent the team from coming. He fights the relationship between the team and the local churches. This is why prayer is such an important part of apostolic ministry. Prayer helps neutralize the opposition of the enemy and releases the plans and purposes of God for the church.

Eternal rewards will come to the team that invests and ties itself to local churches.

---

25. The glory and joy of the apostolic team

The local church becomes the team's glory and joy.

> For what is our hope, or joy, or crown of rejoicing? Are not even ye in the presence of our Lord Jesus Christ at his coming? For ye are our glory and joy.
>
> —1 Thessalonians 2:19–20

> Therefore, my brethren dearly beloved and longed for, my joy and crown, so stand fast in the Lord, my dearly beloved.
>
> —Philippians 4:1

The team glories in the growth and health of the local church. The church becomes the team's joy and crown. Eternal rewards will come to the team that invests and ties itself to local churches. The team rejoices over the church as a father does over his son.

26. The concern of the apostolic team

The apostolic team will seek to further establish and comfort the local churches.

> And sent Timotheus, our brother, and minister of God, and our fellowlabourer in the gospel of Christ, to establish you, and to comfort you concerning your faith.
>
> —1 Thessalonians 3:2

The team will seek to return for further ministry. This is for the purpose of establishing and comforting the churches. Paul sent Timothy to do this when he could not come himself. Satan's attacks on church plants and local churches are countered by the visit of the apostolic team.

27. The follow up of the apostolic team

The apostolic team will follow up on the condition of the local churches.

> For this cause, when I could no longer forbear, I sent to know your faith, lest by some means the tempter have tempted you, and our labour be in vain.
>
> —1 Thessalonians 3:5

> But I trust in the Lord Jesus to send Timotheus shortly unto you, that I also may be of good comfort, when I know your state.
>
> —Philippians 2:19

The team checks up on the condition of the local churches. This is important because we don't want our labor to be in vain. The team is always aware of Satan's attempt to destroy the work of God. The team monitors the condition of the churches they minister in.

28. The life of the apostolic team

The apostolic team's life becomes connected to the churches they minister in.

> For now we live, if ye stand fast in the Lord.
> —1 Thessalonians 3:8

This is a powerful verse of Scripture. Paul is basing his very life on the health of the church. I am reminded the words of Judah concerning the relationship between Jacob and Benjamin: "...seeing that his life is bound up in the lad's life" (Gen. 44:30). The apostle's life is tied to the church. The team becomes one with the churches in which they minister. Their very life is dependent upon the growth and health of the church.

The apostolic team does not come to duplicate what the local leadership has already accomplished. They come to perfect the areas of lack in the church.

---

29. The goal of the apostolic team

The apostolic team perfects that which is lacking in the faith of the saints.

> Night and day praying exceedingly that we might see your
> face, and might perfect that which is lacking in your faith?
> —1 Thessalonians 3:10

The apostolic team does not come to duplicate what the local leadership has already accomplished. They come to perfect the areas of lack in the church. *To perfect* means "to complete." Local churches can lack in the areas of praise and worship, deliverance, prophecy, prayer, prosperity, love, faith, and evangelism. The team can identify the areas of lack and minister in these areas. The apostolic team will help perfect the saints (Eph. 4:11–12).

30. The love of the apostolic team

The apostolic team's love continues to increase toward the local churches.

> And the Lord make you to increase and abound in love one toward another, and toward all men, even as we do toward you.
>
> —1 THESSALONIANS 3:12

The team's love for the local church continues to grow in time. The relationship becomes stronger. Strong relationships are forged between the team and the local church. This opens the way for even more trust and impartation. The greater the love for the church, the more effective the ministry.

Churches that receive the apostolic team will be upgraded in current truth and revelation.

---

31. The revelation of the apostolic team

The apostolic team brings an understanding of the mysteries of God to the local church.

> Let a man so account of us, as of the ministers of Christ, and stewards of the mysteries of God.
>
> —1 CORINTHIANS 4:1

The apostolic team releases revelation to the local churches. The teams act as stewards of the mysteries of God. As churches receive the apostolic team, they will increase in wisdom, knowledge, and understanding. It is given unto us "to know the mysteries of the kingdom" (Matt. 13:11). Apostles are sent to preach the kingdom of heaven (Matt. 10:7).

Churches that receive the apostolic team will be upgraded in current truth and revelation. Releasing revelation is a major function of apostolic ministry (Eph. 3:1–4).

32. The report of the apostolic team

The apostolic team reports back to the church from where they were sent.

> And thence sailed to Antioch, from whence they had been recommended to the grace of God for the work which they fulfilled. And when they were come, and had gathered the church together, they rehearsed all that God had done with them, and how he had opened the door of faith unto the Gentiles.
>
> —ACTS 14:26–27

This is an encouragement to the sending church. The team is the extension of the sending church. There is a spiritual connection between the two. Both work together to advance the kingdom of God. After the fulfillment of the task, the apostolic team returns to the local church until they leave again. They may be sent out for new endeavors or simply desire to return to the churches they helped or established.

The apostolic team must honor and respect the presbytery of a local church. They must never undermine the authority of the local presbytery. However, the local presbytery must receive and honor the input of the apostolic team if they desire to be blessed through its ministry. Jonathan David says:

> The apostolic teams can help open new areas in the spirit dimension for prayer, warfare, worship, or the operation of the gifts. These new avenues of ministry will release fresh

spirit measure into the lives of the believers and drastically affect the spiritual atmosphere over the local church. The apostolic team can release new revelation of truth, prophetic insight, and the operation of the gifts for miracles and healings. This will add to the local work an inheritance of spirit momentum and power. The visit of the apostolic team refreshes, revitalizes and repositions the local churches for more effective ministry.

33. The intercession of the apostolic team
The apostolic teams continue to pray for the local churches.

> Paul, and Silvanus, and Timotheus, unto the church of the Thessalonians which is in God the Father and in the Lord Jesus Christ: Grace be unto you, and peace, from God our Father, and the Lord Jesus Christ. We give thanks to God always for you all, making mention of you in our prayers; Remembering without ceasing your work of faith, and labour of love, and patience of hope in our Lord Jesus Christ, in the sight of God and our Father; Knowing, brethren beloved, your election of God.
> —1 THESSALONIANS 1:1–4

> I thank my God upon every remembrance of you, always in every prayer of mine for you all making request with joy.
> —PHILIPPIANS 1:3–4

There is a bonding between the apostolic team and the local churches they minister in. The apostolic team will remember the church and pray for them. The relationship between the apostolic team and the local church is not casual. There will be a strong covenant bond between the two. These bonds are based on genuine love.

Intercession is a major part of apostolic ministry. Apostolic praying helps release local churches into new realms of glory and power.

34. The need of the apostolic team

The local churches should be encouraged to pray for the apostolic team. The team needs the prayers of the churches.

> Brethren, pray for us.
>
> —1 THESSALONIANS 5:25

> Finally, brethren, pray for us, that the word of the Lord may have free course, and be glorified, even as it is with you.
>
> —2 THESSALONIANS 3:1

The local churches should also pray for the apostolic team. This will open new doors for the team to minister in other regions. The team is strengthened by the prayers of the local churches they minister in. There is a mutual relationship, with each group praying for the other.

35. The respect of the apostolic team

The apostolic team honors and respects leadership. The team will build up the membership of the local church. They will do nothing to demean or lower the leadership in the eyes of the people. They will encourage the saints to esteem the leadership highly.

> And we beseech you, brethren, to know them which labour among you, and are over you in the Lord, and admonish you; And to esteem them very highly in love for their work's sake, and admonish you; and to esteem them very highly in love for their work's sake.
>
> —1 THESSALONIANS 5:12–13

36. The encouragement of the apostolic team

The apostolic team encourages the manifestation of the Holy Spirit.

> Quench not the Spirit. Despise not prophesyings. Prove all
> things; hold fast that which is good.
> —1 THESSALONIANS 5:19–21

The Conybeare translation of verse 19 says, "Quench not [the manifestation] of the Spirit." Spiritual gifts are important in the local church, and they should be encouraged. The apostolic team will help stir up these manifestations. This is especially true concerning prophecy. The Knox translation says, "Do not stifle the utterances of the Spirit." The New English Bible says, "Do not stifle inspiration."

The apostolic team will place honor on the gift of prophecy. The Knox translation of 1 Thessalonians 5:20 says, "Do not hold prophecy in low esteem." Prophecy is to be highly regarded in the church. There is a danger in believers despising prophecy. We are told not to despise prophecy. It is an important gift that edifies and builds up the local assembly. These manifestations will profit the church (1 Cor. 12:7).

The SAMUEL PRINCIPLE

Samuel's was a type of apostolic ministry. His ministry released a fresh wave of the prophetic anointing in Israel. He trained prophets and established a school of prophets. Samuel maintained a circuit of ministry.

> And he went from year to year in circuit to Bethel, and
> Gilgal, and Mizpeh, and judged Israel in all those places.
> —1 SAMUEL 7:16

Samuel established a network for his ministry. Apostolic networks are being birthed around the globe. Apostolic teams are vital to the strength of these networks. Teams can visit the churches in the network and continually upgrade and impart fresh anointing to the network churches. There is also a cross-pollination as different networks relate and draw from one another's strengths.

In addition to planting new churches, the apostolic team can visit and strengthen existing churches. They can develop a circuit of ministry, as Samuel did. This can be done on a yearly basis or by invitation from the churches at certain times. There will also be certain nations that the team will visit on a regular basis in addition to new ones.

Chapter 15

HELPS *and* GOVERNMENTS

And God hath set some in the church, first apostles, second-arily prophets, thirdly teachers, after that miracles, then gifts of healings, helps, governments, diversities of tongues.
—1 CORINTHIANS 12:28

T HE HELPS AND GOVERNMENT MINISTRIES ARE MENTIONED in 1 Corinthians 12:28 after miracles and gifts of healings. They are important to the work of the church. The *helps ministry* needs to be strong in an apostolic church to assist the leadership in carrying out the vision. There are people anointed in the area of helps. They have the grace to assist apostles in carrying out the apostolic mandate. They have authority to help. Their authority must be recognized and released.

Early in the development of our church, we saw the need to release the ministry of helps in the church. The teachings by Buddy Bell were especially helpful. He taught that this is a supernatural ability given by God to assist. These are supportive ministries that hold up the hand of the leaders. This is represented by Aaron and Hur lifting up the hands of Moses (Exod. 17:12).

HELPS MINISTRY *in the* EARLY CHURCH

The apostles recognized the need for helps when they instructed the congregation to choose seven men to assist in ministering to the widows. This freed them to give themselves to prayer and the ministry of the Word (Acts 6:1–7). The result was an increase of the Word of God and a multiplication of disciples. The deacon's ministry is a helps ministry. This ministry needs to be strong in the local church. It has to be strengthened to carry the burden of the local church. Deacons and others in helps ministry need to know their strategic importance in the plan of God. Without them, an apostle will not be able to carry out the vision. Helps is a ministry. This needs to be taught and recognized by the church.

Apostolic churches must be strong in the area of helps, which can include those who stand by and serve the apostle in a very personal way. They know what is needed and help to facilitate the directives of the apostolic leadership. We spent many years teaching in the area of helps and continue to have a regular class in this area. When this anointing is released in a church, the apostle will be free to give himself to prayer and the ministry of the Word.

GOVERNMENT—*the* GIFT *of* ADMINISTRATION

Government, on the other hand, is the gift of administrations. There are people anointed in the area of administrations who have the gift to help organize and facilitate such a large vision. With so much released through the restoration of apostolic ministry, this anointing is a must. This person is anointed to delegate responsibilities and to direct groups of people. They have practical wisdom to help administrate what the apostolic leadership is releasing and establishing. We need to recognize this anointing as an integral part of the church.

Administration must be submitted to the governing anointings of the church. Many denominations and groups of churches have allowed the administrative anointing to become the dominant anointing of the church. Many of these groups are run by administrators. Everything revolves around organization. Every directive comes from headquarters. Many apostolic and prophetic ministries have been killed by administrators. When this anointing supersedes the apostolic anointing, the church will not be able to progress into new things. Apostles need organization, but they cannot be hindered or controlled by it. The organization is made for the apostle, not the apostle for the organization. Organization is meant to help us not control us.

Administrators help us work out the practical aspects of fulfilling the vision. They think in a practical way, which is necessary to get the job done. Everything is not dreams, visions, and revelations. These things set the course, but the gift of government helps bring it into reality. They can design and implement programs that bring the apostle's vision into reality. When this anointing is submitted to the apostle's vision, it will be a blessing to the church. When it is out of position, it will hinder the plan of God. Administrators are not anointed to lead the church; apostles are. They can recommend to the leadership practical ways to carry out the vision.

Administrators help work the details of carrying out the vision. They deal with the small matters that are important to the overall success of the project. This takes a load off of the apostolic leaders. The apostolic leaders can then focus on the overall vision. The administrators also develop and set up the administrative arm of the church. Churches can rise or fall on the strength or weakness of administration.

Everything is not dreams, visions, and revelations.
These things set the course, but the gift of
government helps bring it into reality.

Some leaders are more administrative than others. Some are more visionary. Some are both visionary and administrative. Leaders must have people with strong administrative gifts to help them. The senior leaders cannot become bogged down with too much administration. Some leaders wear themselves down with administration. They experience burnout because they do not recognize others with this gifting, and they do not know how to delegate. Some churches expect pastors to be administrators. They expect the leaders to *be* and to *do* everything.

A vision without administration is like a body without a skeleton. The skeleton holds up the body. Administrations is the bone structure of the church. This is why administrations must be strong in the church.

Some apostolic leaders are very administrative. Axel Sippach of Seattle, Washington, is an apostolic and visionary strategist with a strong gift of administration. He is also one of the apostolic leaders of our I.M.P.A.C.T. Network and has been a tremendous blessing in helping administrate much of what we are doing around the world. Apostle Sippach is gifted in strategizing the plans of God, including how to move, penetrate, and establish the apostolic in certain nations.

However, he still needs those with administrative gifts to help carry out the vision. When he becomes too bogged down with administration, it draws his focus away from the overall vision he has as an apostolic leader. God gives him strategies to impact and affect nations. With the help of the government gift, Axel can be effective in implementing these strategies.

FUNCTIONS *of the* APOSTOLIC MINISTRY

Leaders who are making the transition from a pastoral to an apostolic mode need to understand the functions of the apostolic ministry. This gifting will necessitate strong helps and governments. Some apostolic anointings function differently from pastoral anointings. The duties of the apostle that need to be executed and carried out are numerous. When leaders understand the various functions of this ministry, they will be able to fully move into it, and there will be a grace to fulfill these functions and faithfully carry them out. The following are some of the functions of apostles:

1. Apostles pioneer.

2. Apostles plant churches.

3. Apostles ordain elders.

4. Apostles reform and bring change.

5. Apostles teach, preach, and set doctrine.

6. Apostles release revelation concerning the plans and purposes of God.

7. Apostles raise up and establish teams.

8. Apostles oversee churches.

9. Apostles confirm and strengthen local churches.

10. Apostles bring judgment and correction.

11. Apostles defend the faith.

12. Apostles gather.

13. Apostles establish.

14. Apostles lay foundation.

15. Apostles root out, tear down, throw down, destroy, build, and plant.

16. Apostles water.

17. Apostles bless the poor.

18. Apostles help perfect the saints.

19. Apostles release and activate.

20. Apostles impart.

21. Apostles help release the fullness of the Holy Spirit.

22. Apostles bring strategies to the church.

23. Apostles operate in signs, wonders, and miracles.

24. Apostles declare and decree.

25. Apostles remit sins.

Apostles must operate in faith and know that they are anointed to carry out the different functions of this ministry. This will cause them to expand and launch out into a broader and wider sphere of ministry. More people will be influenced and blessed by the anointing that is released through an apostolic ministry. It is a stronger anointing that carries a greater degree of power and authority. As the apostle steps into this ministry by faith, there will be new dimensions of grace made available. *Apostles must surround themselves with a strong team that includes helps and governments.*

The gifts of God operate by faith. The more confidence and faith a person walks in, the more manifestations of the Spirit he or she will experience. Doubt and passivity will prevent you from walking in the fullness of your calling. Most ministers live and die without entering into all the phases of their ministry. Instead of exceeding their boundaries, many never explore and possess their God-given perimeters. Their gifts will be dormant until stirred up by faith (2 Tim. 1:6).

> Enlarge the place of thy tent, and let them stretch forth the
> curtains of thine habitations: spare not, lengthen thy cords,
> and strengthen thy stakes; For thou shalt break forth on

the right hand and on the left; and thy seed shall inherit the
Gentiles, and make the desolate cities to be inhabited.

—Isaiah 54:2–3

Apostles must surround themselves with a strong team that includes helps and governments.

Enlarge Your Tent

This is a prophetic word for this hour: it is time to "enlarge the place
of thy tent" (Isa. 54:2). Your tent represents your area of ministry. It
is time to lengthen your cords and strengthen your stakes. God is
calling you to a greater area of ministry. The areas mentioned in this
book must be strengthened in the local church. It is up to the leaders
to do the enlarging.

To enlarge means "to increase the capacity or scope of." It means
"to expand." Too many leaders are confining themselves to the four
walls of a local church. Many will die within those walls if they
do not enlarge. The move from the pastoral to the apostolic is an
enlargement. It is an expansion that will result in a greater capacity
to receive and handle all that God is releasing. Many ministries are
about to break forth on both sides. They will not be able to handle
this breaking forth if they do not make room.

Our spirits must be enlarged. Our visions must increase. The
apostolic anointing always enlarges and stretches the vision of the
church. This office will challenge and stir leaders to do more. It will
expand your borders and extend your line throughout the earth (Ps.
19:4). It will break the limitations of culture and tradition, and it will
launch leaders beyond their present boundaries.

> For he that hath, to him shall be given: and he that hath not,
> from him shall be taken even that which he hath.
>
> —Mark 4:25

God is releasing more to those who have revelation and are willing to make the shift. Those who refuse to change will lose what they have. Shifting and changing is necessary if we are to continue to walk in the blessing of God.

As I travel and minister to leaders and churches around the world, I am excited to see what is happening in the lives of leaders and members alike. We have been ordaining leaders as apostles in several different nations. Ordination by man is not necessary to function as an apostle. However, many leaders need the confirmation and recognition by proven apostolic leaders. Jesus ordained the Twelve (Mark 3:14). There will be apostles who ordain and release other apostles. This helps to release and thrust them into the call.

> Those who refuse to change will lose what they have. Shifting and changing is necessary if we are to continue to walk in the blessing of God.

This is an exciting time to be alive! God is breaking the limitations off of our lives and releasing us into our destinies! My desire is to see leaders and churches come into the fullness of what God has ordained. Let us not live beneath our privilege. Let us rise up and embrace everything that our Lord died and shed His blood to purchase for us. We will bring pleasure to God and displeasure to the devil. May grace and peace be multiplied unto the church of Jesus Christ!

Chapter 16

RELEASING EVANGELISTS
and WORSHIP

And the angel of the Lord spake unto Philip, saying, Arise,
and go toward the south unto the way that goeth down from
Jerusalem unto Gaza, which is desert.

—Acts 8:26

Evangelists are not intended to be stuck in the
government of the church. They need to be free to minister to
the lost, as the pastors are free to minister to the sheep. The church
has had less of a problem recognizing and releasing evangelists than
is has had releasing apostles and prophets. Evangelists were not a
threat to most pastors because they were a traveling ministry. The
church also believed in the ministry of the evangelist as one viable
for today. The apostles and prophets have not fared as well.

Evangelists will help bring in the harvest. Evangelists need to be
connected to apostolic churches. Apostolic churches are structured to
be able to handle and maintain the harvest that comes through evangelism. Philip the Evangelist called for the apostles to come to Samaria
after seeing an evangelistic breakthrough. It is not enough to see people

saved. They must be baptized in the Holy Spirit and incorporated into the church. The apostles came to lay hands on the believers to be filled with the Holy Spirit (Acts 8:17). The apostles can teach, train, and impart to the new believers after the evangelist leaves.

Some have called the evangelist *God's paratrooper.* Like Philip, he can drop in suddenly on people, do his job, and be carried away to another assignment (Acts 8:27–40). The evangelist is unpredictable; even the devil does not know where he will turn up next. In this way, he continually keeps the devil on the defensive. The evangelist can do much damage to the kingdom of darkness in a short period of time.

> ### Evangelists need to be connected to apostolic churches. Apostolic churches are structured to be able to handle and maintain the harvest that comes through evangelism.

There are many evangelists sitting in our pews who need to be released. The apostle's vision should be large enough to incorporate and release them into the vision of the church. They need to be recognized, ordained, and released. Their ministries will be more fruitful if they are recognized and released by apostles. The evangelist is also given for the perfecting of the saints. They will help release an evangelistic spirit into the church. They should also operate in an apostolic dimension by receiving the impartation available in the church. Their vision will also be apostolic. They will not be limited by the traditional concept of what it means to be an evangelist. They will operate in a higher level of revelation and power.

Philip the evangelist came out of an apostolic community in Jerusalem and saw great breakthrough in Samaria. He ministered with an apostolic spirit. He was able to go into an area controlled by witchcraft and break through. He pioneered evangelism into a new area. We need pioneering evangelists to be a part of breaking into new regions and territories.

Apostles have the grace to release these gifts. God is the One who gives these gifts by His grace. The pastoral structure of many churches today hinders evangelists from functioning. An apostolic vision is large enough to embrace them all. Furthermore, the apostle recognizes the need for these gifts. The vision is too large to complete without them. They should teach the church their importance and place within the church. Apostles stir evangelists through preaching and teaching and help release them by faith. Evangelists must not draw back because of fear and tradition. They cannot wait for others but must be willing to pioneer if necessary. They must trust in the grace of God to get the job done. Evangelists must be willing to suffer persecution and misunderstanding from religious people for the sake of establishing the truth. They must build by revelation not tradition.

We need to see the restoration of apostolic evangelists. These are evangelists sent out of apostolic houses with apostolic power and authority. These evangelists will work with apostles and other gifts to bring in the harvest. They will have the connection to apostolic houses, like Phillip. Phillip was able to call for the apostles to come after breaking through in Samaria (Acts 8:14–15).

Evangelists can also work with prophets and teachers. This is the concept of apostolic team ministry. I believe when evangelists come into a territory, they should connect with apostles who can help them keep the harvest with follow-up teaching and prophetic ministry.

Evangelists should also be able to prophesy, cast out devils, and pioneer. Evangelists also receive impartation by being a part of an apostolic community. Apostolic evangelists will have a greater capacity to minister more fully to people if they have been around apostolic grace. We are challenging the traditional concept of the evangelist and breaking free from limitations of the past.

We are seeing the release of apostolic reformers. They have the grace and anointing to reform and restructure the church according to the biblical pattern. They will have all the materials they need because of restoration. Apostolic churches will have an abundance of grace. There will be no lack. Evangelists will help bring in the harvest. Once people are saved, they must be brought into an atmosphere of worship. They must encounter and live in the presence of God.

> Apostolic evangelists will have a greater capacity to minister more fully to people if they have been around apostolic grace.

REBUILDING *the* TABERNACLE *of* DAVID THROUGH PROPHETIC WORSHIP

The Second Epistle to the Corinthians is a defense given by Paul concerning his apostolic ministry. He identified this New Testament ministry as a ministry of glory. The people are changed as they come into contact with the glory of God. The apostolic provides an atmosphere of glory for people to come into and be changed.

The church is the habitation of God through the Spirit. The old covenant ark represented the presence of God. David brought this ark and placed it under a tent in Zion. David established Israel's worship in this tabernacle (1 Chron. 25:1–7). The worship was led by three prophetic families. These were the families of Asaph, Heman, and Jeduthun. Each family consisted of prophets and seers who played instruments and sang prophetically. The New Testament church should also be a prophetic family with prophets and those who prophesy by the Holy Spirit (Acts 2:19). What David established in physical Jerusalem was a shadow of what we have in the kingdom.

Once the apostolic and prophetic dimensions are released in a church, the very nature of the church will change. This is especially true in the area of praise and worship. The release of anointed psalmists and minstrels will cause a greater release of God's glory in the church. An open heaven over the ministry will result in a greater liberty in praise and worship. I encourage leaders to do a teaching on the tabernacle of David, which is being restored according to Acts 15:15–19. This tabernacle is a type of the New Testament church. It is also a type of the apostolic. It was a tent erected by David to house the ark of the covenant. Courses of priests were set in place to praise the Lord continually. Many of the psalms were birthed and written during this time. These psalms were prophetic and declared the will and purposes of God.

David was a prophetic psalmist. The church should be prophetic in worship. New songs should be released continually. Every time God does something new, He releases new songs (Isa. 42:9–10). Anointed minstrels release new sounds that move the hand of God (2 Kings 3:15). The development and release of psalmists and minstrels is a key part of restoring the tabernacle of David.

This is why it is so important for churches to be activated prophetically. The singers should be able to prophesy in song. The musicians should be able to prophesy with the instruments. An apostolic culture will embrace the prophetic. Prophecy can either be spoken or sung. Prophetic worship means singing the word of the Lord.

Apostolic churches will be known for the presence of God. There will be a greater liberty and degree of glory in these churches that will affect the spirits of the people. A major part of releasing that glory is the release of anointed psalmists and minstrels. The church must be taught the importance of the manifest presence of God. Believers must know how the presence of God affects and changes a person. Our spirits are impacted and activated as we come into contact with God's glory. The music of the church must be strong and penetrating. The minstrels who have been exposed to the apostolic anointing will have a liberty and strength to release the proper sounds that bring deliverance and move the hand of God. The music cannot be weak, religious, and traditional. We are not building traditional churches but prototype churches.

This is an important part of training and strengthening the spirits of the people. When the spirits of the people are activated and opened up through anointed praise and worship, they will be in a position to receive and understand the revelation that God is releasing. Their spirits will be activated and tuned to a higher frequency. They will be able to receive and walk in deeper truth. They will be able to handle the strong meat of the Word.

Believers must know how the presence of God affects and changes a person. Our spirits are impacted and activated as we come into contact with God's glory.

Apostolic churches will also be known by their liberty. The restraints of religion and tradition are broken. Dancing, praising, shouting, and celebrating are normal. Prophetic utterances are released. New songs are birthed and sung. People are free to enjoy and experience the presence of God. Praise and worship is not just a song service to allow extra time for all the people to arrive or to prepare to hear a twenty-minute sermon. Praise and worship must be a vital part of the church.

The people will experience what it is to live under an open heaven. The apostolic anointing has the ability to open the heavens and keep them open. Apostles have a grace to connect with heaven's resources and pull them down to the earth for ministry function. It is refreshing to live under an open heaven. The church becomes the gate of heaven (Gen. 28:17). Through this gate, the Lord pours His blessings upon the people.

Our church was radically affected by the ministry of Pastor Tom

Bynum. His prophetic psalmist anointing helped release us into a new dimension of praise and worship. Before meeting Tom, we did not know much about spontaneous worship. We received a great amount of impartation from him, and we will always be thankful to him for his gift and sacrifice.

Leaders cannot be satisfied with traditional singing and the usual praise and worship. We must be a part of the rebuilding of the tabernacle of David. David released prophetic priests to be in charge of the worship (1 Chron. 25:1–5). Apostles are anointed to establish. David established the order of worship for the nation of Israel. Although an Old Testament man, he was able to taste the powers of the age to come (Heb. 6:5). David was able to receive a revelation from heaven and establish it upon the earth.

APOSTOLIC CHURCHES ARE JUDAH CHURCHES

As I explained in a previous chapter, *Judah* means "praise." These churches will have their hand in the neck of the enemy. They will carry a scepter of authority (Gen. 49:8–10). The people will gather into these churches because of the open heaven and glory that results. The results of rebuilding the tabernacle of David will be possessing the land and the nations seeking God (Amos 8:11–12).

> **Apostolic people are worshipers. They draw their strength from the presence of God. They love the presence of God. They love dwelling in Zion.**

An apostolic culture is a culture of worship. The prophetic anointing increases the level of worship in a church. This is why we emphasize the establishment of the prophetic ministry within apostolic houses. The kingdom is also connected to worship. We are now living in the age of the kingdom, and the nations have been called to worship (Ps. 22:27–28). The tabernacle of David has been restored. We now live and worship under the tent of David through Christ, the greater David.

Worship in the kingdom is done by spirit and truth. The kingdom is spiritual, the church is a spiritual house, and the church consists of spiritual people who offer spiritual sacrifices. We have come to Zion, the mountain of God. We have come to Zion, the habitation of God. We drink of the river that flows from Zion. This is new covenant worship. This is prophetic worship. This is the new wineskin that holds the new wine.

Apostolic people are worshipers. They draw their strength from the presence of God. They love the presence of God. They love dwelling in Zion. They minister from the strength of Zion. They rule and reign with Christ in Zion. The culture of the church should be apostolic. We are sent ones with a commission and purpose. Living in the apostolic is living in purpose. As the church moves more and more in apostolic power, we will see a greater kingdom expansion from generation to generation. May the Lord stir your heart to believe for greater things in the years to come. Shalom.

Chapter 17

APOSTOLIC CHARACTER

Character is the sine qua non for qualifying and ministering as an apostle.

—C. PETER WAGNER

AN APOSTOLIC CULTURE IS A CULTURE OF HOLINESS AND righteousness. There is sometimes an emphasis on gifting without a corresponding emphasis on character. Apostolic people should be people of exceptional character. Unto whom much is given much is required. Apostolic leaders should develop people of character through teaching and modeling.

This portion of the book will help believers identify true apostolic leaders. People will always reflect the values of their leaders. Leaders set the tone for the church, and they carry a greater responsibility to model godly character.

With the current restoration of apostolic ministry to the church, it is necessary to have biblical standards that believers can measure against those with apostolic claims. The signs of an apostle can include signs, wonders, miracles, church planting, team building, and prophetic confirmation. This is only half of the equation. The other half is apostolic character. Character is often overlooked as a true sign of apostolic ministry.

Ministry not only flows out of gifting but also out of character. Character affects ministry in a vital way. Character shapes the way a person ministers the gifts. Character affects the way the gift is received. A lack of character will sidetrack and hinder the restoration of apostolic gifts to the church. Those who claim apostleship must be able to withstand the test in the area of their character. The enemy will attempt to bring reproach to the apostolic ministry unless the church rises up and enforces biblical standards to those who claim apostleship.

> To overlook character at the expense of power
> is to make a tragic mistake. Apostles must be
> known for their character as well as their acts.

Character includes integrity, honesty, honor, courage, strength, respectability, uprightness, morality, goodness, truthfulness, and sincerity. Character is the badge, sign, seal, mark, trademark, stamp, and signet of a true apostle. Character is what validates the apostolic ministry. An apostolic ministry cannot be confirmed and validated without apostolic character.

> But thou hast fully known my doctrine, manner of life, purpose, faith, longsuffering, charity, patience.
> —2 Timothy 3:10

> Brethren, be followers together of me, and mark them which walk so as ye have us for an ensample.
> —Philippians 3:17

The Acts of the Apostles is a tremendous book that records the deeds of the early apostles and the early church. It is a book of action. Apostles are known for their acts, including miracles, signs, wonders, healings, church planting, evangelism, preaching, and teaching. Apostles walk in tremendous power and authority. They are sent ones who represent God in a unique way. Jesus set the standard for ministry and imparted the same power and authority to the Twelve. With the emphasis on apostolic power, the need for apostolic character is sometimes overlooked. Sent ones are known for what they do and for who they are. To overlook character at the expense of power is to make a tragic mistake. Apostles must be known for their character as well as their acts.

Apostolic leaders are to model apostolic character. They are examples for the church to follow. This is the responsibility of apostles because they have been set "first" in the church. The apostles were the most visible ministries in the New Testament. Their lives must be reflected of Jesus Christ, the Sender. The apostle's character is seen by all.

The first two things Paul mentions in 2 Timothy 3:10 are his doctrine and manner of life. Paul talked about his manner of life. He was not afraid to use his life as a model for others to follow. He was not ashamed of his lifestyle. His manner of life was open for all to see. Manner of life is conduct or behavior. Paul's conduct was observed by Timothy. The Phillips translation says, "...you, Timothy, have known intimately..." The Rotherham translation says, "But thou hast closely studied." An apostle's life can be studied closely without fear of exposure of unrighteousness. An apostle's life can be studied by the spiritual sons and daughters.

Character is defined as "a distinctive trait, quality, or attribute." Character deals with the behavior of a person. The way that an apostle behaves is just as important as the way he ministers. Bad behavior will limit the effectiveness of the minister. God has a very high standard for apostolic leadership. Apostles are entrusted with a tremendous amount of power and authority. There must be a corresponding development of godly character in order to be able to carry what the Lord has entrusted.

A standard is a level of excellence, attainment, and the like, regarded as a measure of adequacy. God requires excellence in character for apostolic leaders. Excellence is the fact or condition of excelling. It is superiority or surpassing goodness or merit. This means that average character is not enough for apostles. Apostles must have a character that is exemplary and well above average. They must strive for and maintain excellence in character.

True apostles can stand before their followers and say without hesitation, "Imitate me!"

Much of the development of emerging apostles is in the area of character. The development of character is an important part of the preparation for an apostolic ministry. There is more to an apostolic ministry than gifting and anointing. The training of apostles requires discipline and correction in the area of character. Jesus spent much time dealing with the character of His disciples.

> Giving no offence in any thing, that the ministry be not blamed: But in all things approving ourselves as the ministers of God.
> —2 CORINTHIANS 6:3–4

> We give no cause for stumbling of any sort, lest our ministry should incur discredit.
> —2 CORINTHIANS 6:3–4, WEYMOUTH

> In fact in everything we do we try to show that we are true ministers of God.
> —2 CORINTHIANS 6:3–4, TAYLOR

Apostolic leaders set the tone for the church. They therefore have a greater responsibility to prove themselves as ministers in the area of character. The apostles were the most up-front and visible ministries in the early church. With the restoration of apostles, they will once again hold a prominent position in the church. Their visibility requires that their character be exemplary. Bad character will cause many to stumble. Apostles must never put a stumbling block in the way of those to whom they are sent.

C. Peter Wagner states, "Apostles have extraordinary character." He maintains that God will not entrust genuine apostolic authority to individuals who have not already attained extraordinary character. In order for apostles, who are regarded as first among Christian leaders (1 Cor. 12:28), to gain the high-ranking spiritual responsibility they are being given, they need to meet the standards for biblical leadership. They can identify with the apostle Paul, who, when answering the objections of some Corinthians to his apostolic authority, wrote, "For I know of nothing against myself" (1 Cor. 4:4, NKJV). These are remarkable words. But only on the basis of such a level of extraordinary character could Paul continue later in the same chapter to say, "Therefore I urge you, imitate me" (1 Cor. 4:16). True apostles can stand before their followers and say without hesitation, "Imitate me!" David Cannistraci states the following:

> How can we determine an apostle's authenticity? Long before we look at charisma, we must examine character. We must strike the touchstone of patience against the character to see if the quality and purity required for apostolic ministry are present.... Without this ingredient in place, the apostle (and the whole apostolic movement) will not endure.

> Even so every good tree bringeth forth good fruit; but a corrupt tree bringeth forth evil fruit. A good tree cannot bring forth evil fruit, neither can a corrupt tree bring forth good fruit....Wherefore by their fruits ye shall know them.
> —MATTHEW 7:17–18, 20

Jesus uses this example when talking about false ministries. A ministry must be judged by its fruit. The Twentieth Century New Testament says, "By the fruit of their lives that ye will know such men." Signs, wonders, and miracles are not the only criteria for true apostolic ministry. We know them by their fruit not by their gifts. An apostolic ministry without the fruit of the Spirit is dangerous to the church. False ministries cannot bring forth good fruit.

> ...that I may know Him and the power of His resurrection, and the fellowship of His sufferings, being conformed to his death.
> —PHILIPPIANS 3:10, NKJV

Jonathan David states the following:

> Today many seek to validate their ministries by pointing out the miracles of healings, the size of their tents, decision cards and somehow it is always their accomplishments that get amplified...In all of the Pauline Epistles there is a clear indication that Paul aspired to be like the Lord Jesus he had encountered at the Damascus road.

In his book *The Radical Church,* Bryn Jones states the following:

> The apostle will be the living example of all that he wants the people to become and do. Therefore, his personal Christlikeness will be evident to all so that they are secure in following his example. He may unashamedly stand before the people and say, "You yourselves know how you ought to follow us" (see 2 Thessalonians 3:7–9). He is humble and a man of prayer. His longsuffering gentleness with the weak, his firmness with those who require it, and his integrity and honesty in business matters and dealings with people should all speak well of him.

And Asa oppressed some of the people the same time.
—2 Chronicles 16:10

But they hearkened not: and Manasseh seduced them to do more evil than did the nations whom the Lord destroyed before the children of Israel.
—2 Kings 21:9

The *apostle* of the New Testament is synonymous with the *king* of the Old Testament. To fully understand the office, ministry, anointing, and purpose of the apostle of the New Testament, we should first familiarize ourselves with and understand the office, ministry, anointing, and purpose of the king of the Old Testament.

God always referred to the character of the king before describing his works. The things kings did always reflected their character. Righteous kings brought great blessing to the people. Ungodly and unrighteous kings brought much trouble to the nation. Ungodly kings were idolatrous and oppressive. They led the people away from the worship of the true God and brought the judgment of God upon the nation.

We are only to submit to godly leadership.
To submit to ungodly leadership is to submit
to control, domination, and witchcraft.

An alleged apostle without the indwelling Holy Spirit; without godly, Christlike character; and behaving and operating apart from Jesus is nothing more than a resurrected, prideful, rebellious, disobedient, stubborn, evil, wicked, and self-willed Old Testament king.

> Remember them which have the rule over you, who have spoken unto you the word of God: whose faith follow, considering the end of their conversation.
>
> —HEBREWS 13:7

"Conversation" is translated from the Greek word *anastrophe,* meaning "behavior." We are to consider the message and the behavior of those who are in authority over us. We are only to submit to godly leadership. To submit to ungodly leadership is to submit to control, domination, and witchcraft. This is why apostolic character is so important. We cannot follow and imitate an ungodly lifestyle.

Chapter 18

TRAITS *of* TRUE APOSTLES

But in all things approving ourselves as the ministers of God, in much patience, in afflictions, in necessities, in distresses, In stripes, in imprisonments, in tumults, in labours, in watchings, in fastings; By pureness, by knowledge, by long suffering, by kindness, by the Holy Ghost, by love unfeigned, By the word of truth, by the power of God, by the armour of righteousness on the right hand and on the left, By honour and dishonour, by evil report and good report: as deceivers, and yet true; As unknown, and yet well known; as dying, and, behold, we live; as chastened, and not killed; As sorrowful, yet alway rejoicing; as poor, yet making many rich; as having nothing, and yet possessing all things.

—2 CORINTHIANS 6:4–10

P AUL'S SECOND LETTER TO THE CORINTHIANS CONTAINS A defense of his apostleship. Paul mentions his sufferings and character as two aspects of his ministry. His character is represented by pureness, longsuffering, kindness, and love unfeigned. Apostles will often have to defend their apostleship, and godly character will be a part of this defense. People will often attack a ministry based on character. The apostle's ministry is no exception. Apostles must be able to present their lifestyle as a proof of their calling. A lack of godly character will give the enemy an opportunity to slander and accuse a ministry. Let's discover what these character traits should be.

1. Pureness and righteousness

> By pureness...
> —2 CORINTHIANS 6:6

"Pureness" is the translation of the Greek word *hagnotes,* meaning "cleanness" (the state), "blamelessness"; it is from the root word *hagnos,* meaning "clean, innocent, modest, perfect, chaste, and pure." This relates to the morals and lifestyle of an apostle. In all aspects of life and ministry, the apostle is to show cleanness and purity. *Pure* means "to be free from any adulterant; unmixed; free from anything that taints, impairs, infects; free from defects; perfect; faultless; free from sin or guilt; blameless."

> ...with innocence...
> —2 CORINTHIANS 6:6, MOFFATT

> ...with purity...
> —2 CORINTHIANS 6:6, MONTGOMERY

Innocence is freedom from sin or moral wrong, freedom from guile or cunning. To be innocent is to be free from sin, evil, or guilt. This is the standard for the apostolic ministry. Apostles are to be blameless.

> ...by the armour of righteousness on the right hand and on the left.
> —2 CORINTHIANS 6:7

The Phillips translation says, "Our sole defense, our only weapon, is a life of integrity."

Righteousness is the apostle's armor. Righteousness will protect from the slander and reproach of the devil. Apostolic character is a defense against the false accusations of the enemy. We must give no place to the devil. Righteous means to act in a just, upright manner, doing what is right. It means to be morally right, fair, and just.

> He that doeth righteousness is righteous, even as he is righteous.
>
> —1 JOHN 3:7

The Phillips translation says, "The man who lives a consistently good life is a good man, as surely as God is good." Synonyms for *righteousness* include "blamelessness," "goodness," "virtuousness," "holiness," "honor," "purity," "honesty," "integrity," "godliness," and "justness."

Patience is necessary for an apostle to be able to finish the course. Without patience an apostle will not be able to endure hardship.

---

2. Longsuffering and patience

> …by longsuffering…
>
> —2 CORINTHIANS 6:6

"Longsuffering" is from the Greek word *makrothumia,* meaning "forbearance, fortitude, patience, perseverance, and endurance." Fortitude is the strength to bear misfortune and pain calmly and patiently; it means "firm courage." Endurance is the ability to last, to continue; the ability to stand pain, distress, fatigue. Patience is the will or ability to wait or endure without complaint, and it means "steadiness" or "perseverance." To persevere is to continue in some effort or course of action in spite of difficulty or opposition.

This character trait is important in order to endure the suffering and persecution that often comes with the apostolic ministry. Long-suffering gives an apostle the ability to overcome spiritual resistance and opposition. Paul is an example of longsuffering. He was able to endure in spite of a shipwreck, beatings, stonings, and imprisonment.

> Truly the signs of an apostle were wrought among you in all patience, in signs, and wonders, and mighty deeds.
> —2 CORINTHIANS 12:12

"Patience" is from the Greek word *hupomolle*, which means "cheerful (or hopeful), endurance, and constancy." The root word *hupomello* means "to stay under, remain, bear trials, have fortitude, persevere, and suffer."

David Cannistraci states, "Patience embodies the concept of proven character more than any other quality because having patience implies not only character, but a character that has been tested in difficulty and proven over a period of time. Patience is a seal that validates a person's spiritual authenticity."

Patience is mentioned in the same list with righteousness, godliness, faith, love, and meekness (1 Tim. 6:11). Patience is necessary for an apostle to be able to finish the course. Without patience an apostle will not be able to endure hardship. The enemy will take advantage of the lack of patience and eventually cause an apostolic ministry to fail.

3. Kindness

> ...by kindness...
> —2 CORINTHIANS 6:6

"Kindness" is from the Greek word *chrestotes*, which means "usefulness, excellence in character or demeanor, gentleness, and goodness."

Kindness means "to be sympathetic, friendly, gentle, tender-hearted, generous, or cordial." *Gentle* means "not violent, not harsh or rough." *Goodness* is kindness, generosity, benevolence, virtue, and excellence. *Excellence* means "to be outstandingly good of its kind, of exceptional merit, virtue."

Kindness is the way an apostle relates to others. Apostolic relationships should be marked by kindness. Kindness is a characteristic of love. Love is the bond of perfectness. Many leaders claiming apostleship are rude and unkind. Some believe that kindness is a sign of weakness. There is no excuse for being unkind in ministry.

4. Love unfeigned—charity

> ...by love unfeigned.
>
> —2 CORINTHIANS 6:6

> And above all these things put on charity, which is the bond of perfectness.
>
> —COLOSSIANS 3:14

Love unfeigned is unpretending love. It is genuine and sincere love. *Unfeigned* means "to be genuine, real, or sincere." *Feigned* means "pretended or simulated." Apostles cannot be pretentious in the area of love. Love is the bond of perfectness. The Phillips translation says in Colossians 3:14 that love is "the golden chain of all the virtues." The Twentieth Century New Testament says, "It is the girdle which makes all complete." "Charity" is the translation of the Greek word *agape*, which means "the God (godly) kind of love." *Charity* means "benevolence and good will."

First Corinthians 13 lists the traits of charity:

1. Charity suffers long (very patient, very kind)

2. Charity envies not (never boils with jealousy)

3. Charity vaunts not itself (not anxious to impress, makes no parade, never boastful)

4. Charity is not puffed up (not arrogant, not conceited, does not put on airs)

5. Charity does not behave itself unseemly (is never rude, never unmannerly)

6. Charity seeks not her own (never selfish, does not insist on its own way)

7. Charity is not easily provoked (not quick to take offense)

8. Charity thinks no evil (does not keep account of evil)

9. Charity rejoices not in iniquity (takes no pleasure in wrongdoing)

10. Charity rejoices in the truth (always glad when truth prevails)

11. Charity bears all things (no limit to its endurance, bears up under anything)

12. Charity believes all things (always eager to believe the best)

13. Charity hopes all things (hopes under all circumstances)

14. Charity endures all things (ever patient)

Charity (love) gives the apostle the ability to endure betrayal, hurts, disappointments, persecutions, afflictions, and all tests and trials. Love is a part of apostolic character that will cause the apostle to make great sacrifices. Love gives the ability to bear up under any circumstance and pressure.

5. Goodness

> For the fruit of the Spirit is in all goodness and righteous-
> ness and truth.
>
> —EPHESIANS 5:9

"Goodness" is from the Greek word *agathosune,* meaning "virtue
or beneficence." Beneficence is the fact or quality of being kind or
doing good. It is a charitable act or a generous gift. Goodness is associated with giving. Goodness is connected to good works.

> And they sent forth Barnabas....For he was a good man,
> and full of the Holy Ghost and of faith.
>
> —ACTS 11:22, 24

Barnabas was sent from Jerusalem to give input into the new
church at Antioch. Barnabas's character is mentioned. He "was a
good man." This is part of apostolic character. Barnabas was the
Levite who sold his land, brought the money, and laid it at the apostles' feet (Acts 4:36–37). Giving is a part of apostolic character.

Rage and anger are signs of bad character. Apostolic character includes self-control in these areas.

---

6. Humility, meekness, gentleness

> Serving the Lord with all humility of mind...
>
> —ACTS 20:19

"Humility" is from the Greek word *tapeinophrosune,* meaning
"modesty, humility of mind, humbleness of mind." Humility applies
to the way an apostle thinks. Apostles cannot be puffed up in their
minds. This is important because "knowledge puffeth up" (1 Cor. 8:1).

Knowledge is a part of the apostolic ministry. Apostles must be careful not to allow knowledge to "puff up" their minds. Pride is one of the most lethal weapons the enemy will use against apostles.

Apostolic ministry is a ministry of revelation (Eph. 3:1–5). Paul received a thorn in the flesh, the messenger of Satan to buffet him (2 Cor. 12:7). The Lord allowed this demonic attack in order to prevent him from being exalted above measure through the abundance of revelations. Humility is an essential part of the apostolic ministry because of the abundance of revelations that apostles carry and minister to the church.

Apostles are stewards of the mysteries of God. They must be faithful and trustworthy with the revelations that are given to them by the Holy Spirit.

Apostles must not be self-seeking. They must not operate in pride by being guilty of selfish ambition. They must not seek power and position. They must not use worldly tactics to gain influence. These things are motivated by pride and vainglory. Apostles must walk in humility and wait for the Lord's promotion.

> Apostles will be people of humility and will not walk in vanity or self-glory. Because apostles can sometimes be considered great leaders, humility should always be a distinctive quality, personally and publicly.
>
> —TIM EARLY

> Now I Paul myself beseech you by the meekness and gentleness of Christ, who in presence am base among you, but being absent am bold toward you.
>
> —2 CORINTHIANS 10:1

"Meekness" is a translation of the Greek word *praotes,* meaning "gentleness and humility." *Meek* is defined as "patient and mild; not inclined to anger or resentment." Rage and anger are signs of bad character. Apostolic character includes self-control in these areas.

> But we were gentle among you, even as a nurse cherisheth her children.
>
> —1 Thessalonians 2:7

"Gentle" is the Greek word *epios*, meaning "mild or kind; not violent, harsh, or rough." Synonyms for *gentle* include "considerate," "thoughtful," "merciful," "tenderhearted," "harmless," "restrained," "controlled."

> And the servant of the Lord must not strive; but be gentle unto all men, apt to teach, patient, in meekness instructing those that oppose themselves.
>
> —2 Timothy 2:24-25

Strife is the act or state of fighting or quarreling. Strife is bitter conflict or struggle. Apostolic character is free from strife. Strife and contention have no place in an apostolic ministry. Strife breeds anger, hatred, bitterness, competition, jealousy, and cruelty. Gentleness is a characteristic of apostles that will avoid strife. Apostles are not brawlers. They are not contentious or combative.

> I humbled my soul with fasting.
>
> —Psalm 35:13

> ...in fastings often...
>
> —2 Corinthians 11:27

Apostles will be wise to spend time in fasting. Fasting is one of the biblical ways to humble the soul. Paul mentions fasting as a part of his apostolic ministry. Fasting is a biblical way to develop humility, and humility is a key to promotion. The promise of exaltation comes to those who humble themselves.

7. Holiness (sanctification)

Ye are witnesses, and God also, how holily and justly and unblameably we behaved ourselves among you that believe.
—1 Thessalonians 2:10

"Holy" is the Greek word *hagios*, meaning "sacred, pure, or consecrated." Apostles are consecrated to the purposes of God. *Consecrated* means "set apart." Apostles are holy vessels. *Sanctify* means "to make holy, to set apart as holy, consecrate, to make free from sin, and to purify."

The church should not be able to witness anything in an apostle's life that is unclean and unholy. The lifestyle of the apostle must be circumspect. The apostle's life should be clean for all to see. This is the standard for apostles. It is a high standard and cannot be compromised.

Apostles must be holy and promote holiness in the church. They must model holiness and teach holiness. Their lifestyle will support their teaching. The apostolic ministry serves as a standard. Apostles help maintain the biblical standards of holiness and righteousness in the church.

8. Faithfulness

Let a man so account of us, as of the ministers of Christ, and stewards of the mysteries of God. Moreover it is required in stewards, that a man be found faithful.
—1 Corinthians 4:1–2

And I thank Christ Jesus our Lord, who hath enabled me, for that he counted me faithful, putting me into the ministry.
—1 Timothy 1:12

Be thou faithful unto death, and I will give thee a crown
of life.

—REVELATION 2:10

**Apostles are stewards of the mysteries of God.
Apostles must be faithful and trustworthy with the
revelations that are given to them by the Holy Spirit.**

"Faithful" is from the Greek word *pistos*, meaning "trustworthy,
trustful, and marked by or showing a strong sense of duty or
responsibility."

Apostles are stewards of the mysteries of God. A steward must
be faithful and trustworthy with what has been entrusted to him.
Apostles must be faithful and trustworthy with the revelations that
are given to them by the Holy Spirit. Faithfulness is a strong sense of
commitment to a person or a thing. Apostles are committed firstly
to Jesus Christ, committed secondly to the message given to them by
Christ, and committed thirdly to the people to whom they are sent
(by Christ).

I have fought a good fight, I have finished my course, I have
kept the faith.

—2 TIMOTHY 4:7

He that is faithful in that which is least is faithful also in
much: and he that is unjust in the least is unjust also in
much. If therefore ye have not been faithful in the unrighteous mammon, who will commit to your trust the true
riches? And if ye have not been faithful in that which is
another man's, who shall give you that which is your own?
No servant can serve two masters: for either he will hate the
one, and love the other; or else he will hold to the one, and
despise the other. Ye cannot serve God and mammon.

—LUKE 16:10–13

Faithfulness is tested in the area of money. Money is a barometer of a person's character. Lack of faithfulness and integrity in finances is a sign of the lack of godly character. Apostolic character includes integrity in financial dealings as well as trustworthiness with offerings. Apostles will use their time, finances, gifts, and revelations for the correct purposes because of faithfulness. Synonyms for *faithful* include "loyal," "allegiant," "devoted," "incorruptible," "unwavering," "reliable," "trusted," "dependable," "honest," "sincere," and "high-principled." God rewards faithfulness. He expects faithfulness unto death.

> Wherefore, holy brethren, partakers of the heavenly calling, consider the Apostle and High Priest of our profession, Christ Jesus; Who was faithful to him that appointed him, as also Moses was faithful in all his house.
> —HEBREWS 3:1–2

We are told to consider Jesus the *Apostle*. We are to consider His faithfulness. Jesus is the perfect Apostle. He was faithful to represent and speak the words of the Sender. Apostles must faithfully represent Jesus. Jesus sends apostles. They must be faithful to speak His word and do His works. This faithfulness must be exhibited in the midst of persecution and opposition.

Lack of faithfulness and integrity in finances is a sign of the lack of godly character.

The faithfulness of Jesus is compared to the faithfulness of Moses. Moses is also a type of an apostle. Moses was faithful to carry out his mission of delivering and leading Israel out of Egypt. He was also faithful to deliver the Law to Israel. Both Jesus and Moses were leaders with integrity.

9. Temperance

> And every man that striveth for the mastery is temperate in all things.... But I keep under my body, and bring it into subjection: lest that by any means, when I have preached to others, I myself should be a castaway.
>
> —1 CORINTHIANS 9:25, 27

Temperance is self-restraint in conduct. *To be temperate* means "to be moderate in one's actions or speech." Paul knew the possibility of being disqualified. He had a responsibility to control his appetites and subdue his body. Self-control is necessary to be able to continue in an apostolic ministry. This includes periodic fasting. Synonyms for *temperance* include "moderation," "self-restraint," "self-control," "self-denial," and "forbearance."

> He that hath no rule over his own spirit is like a city that is broken down, and without walls.
>
> —PROVERBS 25:28

The Jerusalem translation says, "An open town, and without defenses: such is a man lacking self-control." Walls of ancient cities were for the defense of the town. A town without walls has no defense against an attacking army. The enemy will exploit an apostle who has no self-control. A lack of self-control has been the destruction of many ministries.

Chapter 19

INTEGRITY—*the* BADGE
of a TRUE APOSTLE

Receive us; we have wronged no man, we have corrupted no
man, we have defrauded no man.

—2 Corinthians 7:2

Not one of you has ever been wronged or ruined or cheated
by us

—2 Corinthians 7:2, Phillips

*I*NTEGRITY IS DEFINED AS "THE QUALITY OR STATE OF BEING OF
sound moral principle." It means "uprightness, honesty, and
sincerity." Fred Price states:

A man of integrity takes integrity personally. He is his own
person. He does not do something simply because he sees
other people doing it. He follows the guide that is within
him—not the crowd. He lets this guide, not his circumstances, lead him in developing his ethics. And he has
such character, such intestinal fortitude and self-discipline,
that he will consistently do what he knows is morally right
despite the consequences, That is what it means to be a

person of integrity—and it takes morals, character and ethics, which is why these are inherent in the very meaning of integrity.

Honesty in the area of finances is also an important character trait of apostles. The Word of God has much to say on the handling of money. Many apostles and leaders have failed in this area. The apostle must be able to say, "No one has been cheated by me."

> Providing for honest things, not only in the sight of the Lord, but also in the sight of men.
> —2 Corinthians 8:21

> Pray for us: for we trust we have a good conscience, in all things willing to live honestly.
> —Hebrews 13:18

Honesty is that which will not lie, cheat, or steal; it means "truthful, trustworthy, and gained or earned by fair methods." The Moffatt translation says, "My desire is to be perfectly straight and clean." Synonyms for *honesty* include "upright," "trustworthy," "honorable," "equitable," "legal," and "for all to see." Apostles must live honestly. Good character includes a good conscience.

> But have renounced the hidden things of dishonesty, not walking in craftiness, nor handling the word of God deceitfully; but by manifestation of the truth commending ourselves to every man's conscience in the sight of God.
> —2 Corinthians 4:2

The Goodspeed translation says, "...disgraceful, underhanded ways." The Beck translation says, "We don't use trickery." This includes misusing the Word of God in order to take advantage of people. The Twentieth Century New Testament says, "...refusing to adopt crafty ways, or to tamper with God's message." Synonyms for *deceit* include "deception," "hypocrisy," "trickery," "guile," "slyness," "underhand-edness," and "double-dealing." True apostles have a conscience. They have an awareness of what is right and wrong. Ministers with no conscience are dangerous. A lack of conscience will result in many being hurt and taken advantage of without regret.

> For our exhortation was not of deceit, nor of uncleanness, nor in guile:But as we were allowed of God to be put in trust with the gospel, even so we speak; not as pleasing men, but God, which trieth our hearts.For neither at any time used we flattering words, as ye know, nor a cloke of covetousness; God is witness.
>
> —1 THESSALONIANS 2:3–5

Regardless of how gifted and anointed a person may be, greed for money is a sure sign of a character flaw.

Guile is defined as "slyness, cunning in dealing with others, and craftiness." *Flattery* is defined as "to praise too much" and "to speak untruly or insincerely, in order to win favor." Flattery is used as a cloak to take advantage of a person or a group. Flattery covers up the real intention of greed. Financial gain is not the motive of apostles. They will not use deceitful methods to take advantage of people financially. Like Paul, "I have coveted no man's silver, or gold, or apparel" (Acts 20:33).

Covetous is defined as "being greedy." Greed is a sign of bad character. Regardless of how gifted and anointed a person may be, greed for money is a sure sign of a character flaw. The area of finances is an important area of ministry in which the character of an apostle will be tested. Those who fail the test with money will not be qualified to advance in their callings.

> Yea, they are greedy dogs which can never have enough, and
> they are shepherds that cannot understand: they all look to
> their own way, every one for his gain, from his quarter.
>
> —ISAIAH 56:11

The Spurrell translation says, "…each for his own covetous purposes." *Greedy* means "wanting or taking all one can get, with no thought of the needs of others." Greed is a sign of selfishness.

> Feed the flock of God which is among you, taking the over-
> sight thereof, not by constraint, but willingly; not for filthy
> lucre, but of a ready mind; Neither as being lords over God's
> heritage, but being examples to the flock.
>
> —1 PETER 5:2–3

The Williams translation says, "…not from the motive of personal profit but freely." Flocks are not to be considered financial opportunities. The motive of apostles must not be financial gain. Apostles are motivated by their commissions. Apostles should not be driven by money. The apostle is to be an example to the flock. They must be examples in the area of character. They are to be models that can be copied.

**Apostles do have the right to financial support.
They can forego that right if it hinders the message
they preach. Their commitment to the message
given to them is to be their foremost concern.**

The lifestyle of an apostle must be seen as an example of Christ-like character. Apostles are not to be controlling and dominating over the flock. Control and domination are signs of false apostles.

> Did I make a gain of you by any of them whom I sent unto
> you? I desired Titus, and with him I sent a brother. Did Titus

make a gain of you? walked we not in the same spirit? walked
we not in the same steps?

—2 CORINTHIANS 12:17–18

The Conybeare translation says, "Did I defraud you of your wealth
by some of the messengers whom I sent to you?" Apostles will not use
schemes and tricks to defraud God's people financially. The ones who
are a part of the apostolic team must also walk in the same spirit. Paul
received no offerings from the Corinthian church, although he had
a right to be supported. He did this in order to differentiate himself
from false apostles who greedily demanded maintenance. Apostles
do have the right to financial support. They can forego that right if it
hinders the message they preach. Their commitment to the message
given to them is to be their foremost concern.

JUDAS ISCARIOT: *The* FAILED APOSTLE

Then saith one of his disciples, Judas Iscariot, Simon's son,
which should betray him, Why was not this ointment sold
for three hundred pence, and given to the poor? This he said,
not that he cared for the poor; but because he was a thief,
and had the bag, and bare what was put therein.

—JOHN 12:4–6

Judas Iscariot is the only example in the Bible of a failure in the
apostolic ministry (Acts 1:17–20). He was numbered with the Twelve
and was sent out to heal the sick and cast out devils. His weakness
was money. The Bible declares that he was a thief. His betrayal of
Jesus was for thirty pieces of silver. Covetousness was his downfall. It
was an open door for Satan to come into him. Although he operated
in the power of God, he lacked the character necessary to sustain his
ministry.

> ...and covetousness, which is idolatry.
>
> —COLOSSIANS 3:5

The Old Testament kings were types of the apostolic ministry. Evil kings were always guilty of idolatry. This equates to covetousness in the New Testament. Evil kings are also types of false apostolic ministry.

> This he said, not that he cared for the poor; but because he was a thief, and had the bag, and bare what was put therein.
>
> —JOHN 12:6

Judas Iscariot was responsible for carrying the bag of money. He was the treasurer. He began stealing from the bag. This lack of integrity opened the door for Satan to control him.

> And supper being ended, the devil having now put into the heart of Judas Iscariot, Simon's son, to betray him.
>
> —JOHN 13:2

Judas allowed his heart to be filled by Satan with the idea of betraying Jesus. Judas allowed this thought into his heart for money. The demon of covetousness opened the way for him to betray the Lord.

> And after the sop Satan entered into him. Then said Jesus unto him, That thou doest, do quickly.
>
> —JOHN 13:27

Satan found an opening and an opportunity to enter Judas. Judas was an apostle. He was chosen by Jesus and numbered with the Twelve. And just like the other eleven, he was sent to preach the gospel, heal the sick, and cast out devils.

> Then one of the Twelve, called Judas Iscariot, went unto the chief priests, And said unto them, what will ye give me, and

I will deliver him unto you? And they covenanted with him for thirty pieces of silver.

—MATTHEW 26:14–15

Judas was already possessed and controlled by Satan when he went to the priests. He had opened the door for Satan through covetousness and was now headed for destruction. He would lose his apostolic ministry and end up in hell. He later realized his mistake and was sorrowful, but by that time it was too late.

Jesus answered them, Have not I chosen you twelve, and one of you is a devil? He spake of Judas Iscariot the son of Simon: for he it was that should betray him, being one of the twelve.

—JOHN 6:70–71

Judas was a thief. He was a devil. He was chosen by Jesus to partake of an apostolic ministry, but he was covetous. His character did not qualify him to continue in an apostolic call and ministry. He never fulfilled his calling because he was a devil. The devil is a thief.

The example of Judas is a sober warning to all apostles of the dangers of covetousness and opening the door for Satan.

Stealing and lying is the nature of the devil. To call someone a devil implies they have his character. The issue is character. Apostles must have the character of Christ. You cannot have the character of the devil and walk in an apostolic ministry. Apostles must beware of covetousness. Covetousness can lead a leader down the road to destruction. The example of Judas is a sober warning to all apostles of the dangers of covetousness and opening the door for Satan.

QUALIFICATIONS *of an* APOSTLE

In 1 Timothy 3:1–7, Paul mentions the qualifications of a bishop to Timothy, who was acting in an apostolic capacity in setting leadership in the local church. Apostles are overseers (bishops, elders), and these qualifications would also apply to them. This is a part of apostolic character:

1. Blameless (without reproach, no fault can be found, no grounds for accusation)

2. Husband of one wife (not polygamous)

3. Vigilant (temperate)

4. Sober (self-restrained, orderly, serious minded)

5. Good behavior (well-ordered life, disciplined life)

6. Given to hospitality (showing love for and being a friend to believers)

7. Apt to teach (qualified to teach)

8. Not given to wine (neither a drunkard)

9. No striker (not a brawler, not combative)

10. Not greedy of filthy lucre (not covetous)

11. Patient (gentle, peaceable)

12. Not a brawler (not contentious, not quarrelsome)

13. Not covetous (not a lover of money)

14. One that ruleth well his own house (having his children in subjection)

15. Not a novice (not a new convert, not immature)

16. Good report of them who are without (good testimony of those outside the church)

A lack in any of these areas will open the door for the enemy to bring reproach against the ministry. It is interesting to note that the Word mentions striking and brawling, as well as filthy lucre and covetousness. There seem to be double references to similar flaws. Apostles cannot be contentious and greedy of money. These two areas must be clear in order to qualify for apostolic leadership.

Chapter 20

FALSE APOSTLES

I know thy works, and thy labour, and thy patience, and how thou canst not bear them which are evil: and thou hast tried them which say they are apostles, and are not, and hast found them liars.

—Revelation 2:2

For such are false apostles, deceitful workers, transforming themselves into the apostles of Christ.

—2 Corinthians 11:13

Prove all things; hold fast that which is good.

—1 Thessalonians 5:21

T HE EPHESIAN CHURCH WAS COMMENDED FOR TESTING those who claimed apostleship. One of the ways we can test ministers is by testing their fruit. We are to prove all things. Anything God ordains and sends will pass the test. The church is responsible for whom it ordains and receives.

Apostleship is a high calling. There are many today claiming apostleship who do not measure up to the biblical standards of holiness and integrity. Many emerging apostles are still in the process of being trained and refined. There are many true apostles who are of different levels of preparation. The Twelve were not perfect. Jesus had to deal with them as disciples. He especially dealt with the area of ambition.

There is a time between calling and sending that is known as preparation. The call of God is upon many today. The apostolic calling is evident in the lives of many. Many have received prophetic words concerning an apostolic calling. God will also give prophetic words concerning training and refining. The preparation time between calling and sending is important. During this time, God deals with the character and maturity of an emerging apostle. He especially deals with the area of faithfulness. Barnabas and Saul taught faithfully in the church at Antioch before being released into the apostolic ministry. The character of the apostle must be proven before the apostle is fully released.

We are to test those who claim apostleship.
We must accept the true and reject the
false. Character is one of the measuring
lines that we use to determine the true.

The church often overlooks character because of gifting, but the true character of a minister will eventually come forth; if the character is bad, the church will suffer. You cannot hide character. It will be revealed under pressure. What is in the heart will manifest. That which is hidden will come out into the open. Character cannot be ignored. To ignore character at the expense of gifting will have disastrous results. Apostolic character is the trademark of the true church. The church is to be apostolic in nature. This includes apostolic character.

C. Peter Wagner states the following:

Let's agree that apostles are expected to be further up the scale toward perfection than other believers. Why do I say this? It is because God has a double standard of judgment. I know this will surprise some, but just consider what the Bible is saying in James 3:1: "My brethren, let not many of you become teachers, knowing that we shall receive a stricter judgment." Another way of putting this is that God has one standard of judgment for leaders and another for the rest of the Body of Christ. Teachers are used as an example of leaders in James. But 1 Corinthians 12:28 says: "And God has appointed these in the church: first apostles, second, prophets, third teachers." If teachers face a stricter judgment, it follows that apostles will be judged even more strictly. Apostles are apostles, not because they are perfect, but partly because they have met God's standards of holiness and humility.

Apostles are therefore known for their extraordinary character. Character is one of the things that will stand out with a true apostle. It will be a signet. It is a part of the apostolic seal. Character will be a visible and notable mark of a true apostle. It should be one of their outstanding characteristics. Leaders will receive a greater judgment. There is a different standard for leaders. Unto whom much is given, much is required. Apostles must walk in a standard of holiness and righteousness that is higher.

THE UNSENT ONES

There are those who claim apostleship because of its benefits and authority. Some like the position and power of the apostle's ministry. They covet the position. They transform themselves into apostles of Christ. *Transform* is from the Greek word *metaschematizo*, meaning "to transfigure" or "disguise." *To disguise* means "to hide the real nature of." The real nature of false apostles is hidden. They are pretending. They have not been called, not been prepared, nor sent. They are operating in the strength of the flesh and not in the anointing of the Holy Spirit. Their character and lifestyle is not in line with their message. We are to test those who claim apostleship. We must accept the true and reject the false. Character is one of the measuring lines that we use to determine the true. Here are some of the character flaws that the Word identifies in a false apostle.

False apostles bring people into bondage.

> For ye suffer, if a man bring you into bondage, if a man devour you, if a man take of you, if a man exalt himself, if a man smite you on the face.
>
> —2 Corinthians 11:20

> You tolerate a man even when he enslaves you...
>
> —2 Corinthians 11:20,
> Twentieth Century New Testament

> Why, you let other people tyrannize over you...
>
> —2 Corinthians 11:20, Knox

> ...if a man takes away your liberty...
>
> —2 Corinthians 11:20, Phillips

False apostles enslave and demand to be served. Paul wrote the second letter to the Corinthians to defend his apostleship. In so doing, he exposed those who claimed apostleship but were not sent. The Corinthians were receiving false ministers and rejecting the true apostolic ministry of Paul. They were tolerating those who were enslaving them.

Many leaders either knowingly or unknowingly practice charismatic witchcraft. This is using the gifts of God to control and manipulate people. Witchcraft is using fleshly and demonic power to control the lives of members of a church. Some members have had curses placed upon them by leadership when they left a ministry.

Many are so fearful of leaving that they never leave, although they know and see the control of the leadership. Many need deliverance from spirits of witchcraft, control, and fear. This is because they have been brought into bondage.

True apostles are servants. They do not attempt to dominate the faith of others. False apostles will operate in control and domination.

The Galatian church had been bewitched (Gal. 3:1). They had come under the spell and control of false ministers. This is always a danger, and this is why we need true apostles to confront and deal with these issues. Believers need to be able to discern the difference between the false and the true.

The opposite was true of Paul's ministry. He did not act in a controlling way. True apostles are servants. They do not attempt to dominate the faith of others. False apostles will operate in control and domination. The Wuest translation of 2 Corinthians 11:20 says, "For you tolerate a man, if, as is the case, he brings you to the point of abject slavery." Synonyms for *slavery* include "captivity," "oppression," "subjugation," "domination," "control," "subordination," and "servitude."

False apostles devour.

> ...if a man devour you...
>
> —2 CORINTHIANS 11:20

The second thing Paul notes about false apostles is that they "devour you." The Twentieth Century New Testament says, "...when he plunders you." The Phillips translation says, "...spends your money." False apostles are greedy and covetous. The love of money is a characteristic of false ministry. False apostles will greedily demand maintenance. Again, the issue is money. Apostolic character will have integrity with financial issues.

False apostles take advantage.

> …if a man take of you…
>
> —2 CORINTHIANS 11:20

The third thing Paul mentions is "if a man take of you." The Knox translation says, "…take advantage of you." False apostles prey upon the church. They will take advantage of the saints. This means they will use whatever power they have to benefit themselves. This grieves the Holy Spirit. God loves His people and desires them to receive true ministers who will bless and perfect them.

False apostles exalt themselves.

> …if a man exalt himself…
>
> —2 CORINTHIANS 11:20

The fourth thing Paul mentions is "if a man exalt himself." The Twentieth Century New Testament says, "…when he puts on airs of superiority." The Knox translation says, "…vaunt their power over you." False apostles will exalt themselves over the people. They are proud and arrogant. This is the opposite of true apostolic ministry, which is humble and meek. False apostles will make you feel small and unworthy.

A bad tree cannot bring forth good fruit. True apostles will edify and build up. False apostles will beat up and tear down.

False apostles are abusive.

> ...if a man smite you on the face...
>
> —2 Corinthians 11:20

The fifth thing Paul mentions is "if a man smite you on the face." This represents abuse. False apostles are rude and abusive. *To abuse* means "to beat, to hit, to strike, to wound, and to misuse." False apostles beat the saints with their sermons. The issue is character. False apostles cannot manifest godly character. A bad tree cannot bring forth good fruit. True apostles will edify and build up. False apostles will beat up and tear down. To smite in the face is a misuse of authority. Apostolic authority is given for edification, not destruction. (See 2 Corinthians 10:8; 13:10.)

False apostles are greedy and exploitative.

> And many shall follow their pernicious ways....And through covetousness shall they with feigned words make merchandise of you.
>
> —2 Peter 2:2–3

This is Peter's definition of false ministry. The Berkeley translation says, "Motivated by greed, they will exploit you with their counterfeit arguments." These teachers do not speak the truth. They speak contrary to the Word of God. They seduce and manipulate with their words. *Pernicious* means "lascivious, licentious, wanton, and immoral." False apostles are immoral. This is often in the sexual area. It is also true with regard to money. Perversion, adultery, and homosexuality are rampant among false ministers.

> But chiefly them that walk after the flesh in the lust of uncleanness, and despise government. Presumptuous are they, selfwilled, they are not afraid to speak evil of dignities....Having eyes full of adultery, and that cannot cease

from sin; beguiling unstable souls: an heart they have exercised with covetous practices; cursed children.

—2 PETER 2:10, 14

Peter mentions lust, rebellion, self-will, covetousness, and evil
speaking as the signs of a false ministry. Presumptuousness and
self-will represent arrogance and headstrongness. I would like to
emphasize the area of sexual impurity. The Weymouth translation
says, "…especially those who are abandoned to sensuality." Sexual
purity is an important part of apostolic character. Adultery and
fornication have no place in an apostolic leader's life.

False apostles are like wolves.

Beware of false prophets, which come to you in sheep's
clothing, but inwardly they are ravening wolves.

—MATTHEW 7:15

Wolves have insatiable appetites. They represent false ministries.
To be ravenous means "to be greedy and eager for gratification."
Wolves hunt their prey and devour them. False ministries disguise
themselves as sheep, but inwardly they have the nature of a wolf.

True apostles are models in lifestyle and
speech. They manifest sound speech
that cannot be condemned.

False apostles are malicious with their words.

Malicious means "to be intentionally harmful." The word *malice*
means "to have ill will and the desire to hurt another." It also means
"to be spiteful or vindictive." Malice toward others is caused by a
heart filled with envy, jealousy, and bitterness. False apostles speak
evil against others and are very abusive with their tongues. They are

disrespectful to authority. Their speech includes ridicule, mockery, and criticism. Diotrephes was a leader in the church who was disrespectful to the apostolic authority of John. What was in his heart came through the abusive words against authority. It is impossible for evil men to speak good things.

> O generation of vipers, how can ye, being evil, speak good things? for out of the abundance of the heart the mouth speaketh. A good man out of the good treasure of the heart bringeth forth good things: and an evil man out of the evil treasure bringeth forth evil things.
>
> —MATTHEW 12:34–35

The following sins of the tongue are common among false apostles:

1. *Boasting*—to talk proudly about deeds, abilities, etc. Boasting is rooted in pride and arrogance.

2. *Railing*—speaking vilification, blasphemy, evil

3. *Cursing*—calling down evil or injury upon

4. *Lying*—making false statements with the intent to deceive

5. *Exaggeration*—speaking and magnifying something beyond the facts

6. *Profanity*—unclean language, coarse jesting, foul speech

7. *Mockery*—a false, derisive, or impertinent imitation

8. *Flattery*—excessive, untrue, or insincere praise

I wrote unto the church: but Diotrephes, who loveth to have the preeminence among them, receiveth us not. Wherefore, if I come, I will remember his deeds which he doeth, prating against us with malicious words...

—3 John 9–10

In all things shewing thyself a pattern of good works: in doctrine shewing uncorruptness, gravity, sincerity, Sound speech, that cannot be condemned...

—Titus 2:7–8

We must listen carefully to the words that come out of the mouths of those who claim apostleship. Do they use their words in a way that is beneficial to the church? Do they use their words to manipulate, deceive, beat, and control?

True apostles are models in lifestyle and speech. They manifest sound speech that cannot be condemned. We are to be examples in both word and deed. Unclean, foul, abusive, and malicious speech is a sign of ungodly character.

My brethren, be not many masters, knowing that we shall receive the greater condemnation. For in many things we offend all. If any man offend not in word, the same is a perfect man, and able also to bridle the whole body.

—James 3:1–2

These are murmurers, complainers, walking after their own lusts; and their mouth speaketh great swelling words, having men's persons in admiration because of advantage.

—Jude 16

> Now I beseech you, brethren, mark them which cause divisions and offences contrary to the doctrine which ye have learned; and avoid them. For they that are such serve not our Lord Jesus Christ, but their own belly; and by good words and fair speeches deceive the hearts of the simple.
>
> —ROMANS 16:17–18

The words of false ministers are beguiling and deceptive. They lie, flatter, and use smooth words to deceive the hearts of the simple. They take advantage, especially in the area of money, by using words that cover up their real intent.

> Also of your own selves shall men arise, speaking perverse things, to draw away disciples after them.
>
> —ACTS 20:30

False apostles are guilty of perverse speech. *Perverse* means "deviating from what is considered right or good." Perverse speech is crooked speech. This includes false doctrine, heresy, and false teaching. This will also include teachings that divide and separate the church. The tongue is a sure sign of what is inside. We must listen carefully to the words that come out of the mouths of those who claim apostleship. Do they use their words in a way that is beneficial to the church? Do they use their words to manipulate, deceive, beat, and control? Words are carriers of spiritual power. Words can carry God's power or demonic power. False apostles are tools of Satan. They are used to release witchcraft and demonic power that destroy lives and to pervert the true purposes of God.

A TRUE APOSTLE IS EMPOWERED *by the* GRACE *of* GOD

The apostle is a "sent one." Sent ones have lawful power and authority to operate in the spheres to which they are sent. Those who are not sent must use unscrupulous methods to succeed. False ministries do not have the grace to do what a sent one does. Without grace, one must depend upon the flesh to accomplish what can only be done in the Spirit. This will include witchcraft, control, domination, manipulation, intimidation, deception, craftiness, flattery, and seduction.

True apostles do not have to resort to these tactics. They are sent with the necessary grace to accomplish their mission. They do not have to compromise in the area of character. They can depend on and trust in the grace of God to finish the work. They renounce the hidden things of dishonesty. They walk in holiness and integrity. They don't have to use "shortcuts" to arrive at their destination. They can do things legally and righteously and expect the right outcome. People will recognize the grace of a sent one and respond to it. They will follow the anointing that is supported by godly character.

The church should demand that apostles walk in a high standard of character. This will prevent the church from being abused and taken advantage of by bad leadership and false apostles.

Dr. Bill Hamon, the author of *Prophets and the Prophetic Movement,* uses the ten *M*s as a standard for prophets. These ten *M*s can also be applied to apostles. They include:

1. *Manhood*—God makes a man before manifesting mighty ministry.

2. *Ministry*—No offense to ministry

3. *Message*—Speak the truth in love

4. *Maturity*—Attitude right; mature in human relations

5. *Marriage*—Scripturally in order

6. *Methods*—Rigidly righteous, ethical, honest, and integrity

7. *Manners*—Unselfish, polite, kind, a gentleman or lady, and discreet

8. *Money*—Not craving wealth and resorting to ignoble and dishonest methods

9. *Morality*—Virtuous, pure, and proper relationships

10. *Motive*—To serve or to be seen? Fulfill personal drive or God's desire?

Dr. Hamon has been instrumental in helping to release prophets and prophetic churches through his teaching, preaching, and activation. His emphasis has been on gifting and character. It is important that those involved in the apostolic movement also emphasize character. Gifting alone is not sufficient for an apostolic ministry. The ten *M*s should apply to apostles as well as all ministers. The church should demand that apostles walk in a high standard of character. This will prevent the church from being abused and taken advantage of by bad leadership and false apostles.

Chapter 21

PITFALLS *of* APOSTLES

Be sober, be vigilant; because your adversary the devil, as a
roaring lion, walketh about, seeking whom he may devour.

—1 PETER 5:8

As we saw in the previous chapter, apostles may not
be perfect, but they absolutely cannot have character flaws
that cause them to use and take advantage of God's people. They
must have integrity and be submitted to the will of God. Apostles
also have to keep watch against the wiles and attempts of the enemy
against their ministry and anointing. There are four common pitfalls
that Satan has set up to ensnare the apostolic leader.

1. PURPOSE *and* DETERMINATION

Apostles can have strong wills and personalities. Apostles have strong
purpose and determination. This gives them the strength to endure
opposition and overcome the resistance of the enemy. Apostles,
however, must be careful that the enemy does not take advantage of
their will and influence them to go forward into areas that God has
not sent them. I believe this can be seen in the life of Paul. Paul was

warned several times concerning his trip to Jerusalem. He continued in spite of these warnings and almost lost his life. He ended up in prison and went to Rome in chains.

Apostles need the prophetic ministry and should submit to it when necessary. Prophets can provide spiritual help to apostles and warn them concerning upcoming danger.

> And there abode three months. And when the Jews laid wait for him, as he was about to sail into Syria, he *purposed* to return through Macedonia....For Paul had *determined* to sail by Ephesus, because he would not spend the time in Asia: for he *hasted*, if it were possible for him, to be at Jerusalem the day of Pentecost.
>
> —ACTS 20:3, 16, EMPHASIS ADDED

Paul had a purpose and was determined to go to Jerusalem. He hasted to get to Jerusalem, hoping to arrive for the Feast of Pentecost. Apostles have strong purpose and determination, but their purpose and determination must be in line with the will of God. Apostles must be careful what they purpose and determine. *Purpose* is defined as "an aim or goal, a determination or resolution." *Determination* is "firmness of purpose, resolve."

> And now, behold, I go bound in the spirit unto Jerusalem, not knowing the things that shall befall me there: Save that the Holy Ghost witnesseth in every city, saying that bonds and afflictions abide me.
>
> —ACTS 20:22–23

Paul was determined to go to Jerusalem in spite of the witness of the Holy Ghost of bonds and afflictions. Was the Holy Spirit leading him to go to Jerusalem and then preparing him for what would happen? Or was the Holy Spirit trying to keep him from going by warning him of what would happen? If the latter is true, Paul's determination was so strong until he ignored the clear warning of the Holy Spirit. This, if true, is a warning to apostles concerning purpose and determination that the enemy can influence and thus sidetrack them in their ministries.

> And finding disciples, we tarried there seven days: who said to Paul through the Spirit, that he should not go up to Jerusalem.
>
> —ACTS 21:4

This verse is clear. The disciples who Paul met on the way to Jerusalem warned him not to go. This scripture tells us that they spoke through the Spirit. The Holy Spirit would not tell Paul to go to Jerusalem and then warn him not to go. This would be contradictory. Paul's determination caused him to continue on toward Jerusalem.

> And as we tarried there many days, there came down from Judaea a certain prophet, named Agabus. And when he was come unto us, he took Paul's girdle, and bound his own hands and feet, and said, Thus saith the Holy Ghost, So shall the Jews at Jerusalem bind the man that owneth this girdle, and shall deliver him into the hands of the Gentiles. And when we heard these things, both we, and they of that place, besought him not to go up to Jerusalem. Then Paul answered, What mean ye to weep and to break mine heart? for I am ready not to be bound only, but also to die at Jerusalem for the name of the Lord Jesus. And when he would not be persuaded, we ceased, saying, The will of the Lord be done.
>
> —ACTS 21:10–14

Ralph Mahoney has this to say about Paul's trip to Jerusalem:

> Why was the Holy Spirit giving him the same message in every city? Was it because the Holy Spirit wanted to torture him with bonds and afflictions, imprisonment, and chains?

No! When the Holy Spirit starts witnessing that way in your life, it's so you will reconsider your course. You will reconsider your action, and direction, and be saved unnecessary suffering. Everywhere Paul went, the Holy Spirit was witnessing, saying bonds and afflictions awaited him. But Paul remained unmoved by such warnings. He was not going to be deterred. He was going to Jerusalem. Paul had set himself on a course that was not in line with God's perfect will and vision for his life.

Agabus was a recognized prophet in the early church. He used Paul's girdle to demonstrate what would happen to Paul in Jerusalem. Those with Paul tried to persuade him not to go to Jerusalem; Paul's apostolic team tried to persuade him not to go. It is important for apostles to listen to the team. Team members can bring balance to an apostle and help him to make wise decisions. Paul ignored the counsel of his team and remained steadfast in his resolve to go to Jerusalem.

Paul received many witnesses and warnings not to go to Jerusalem. He bypassed these warnings and ended up in Jerusalem. Norman Parrish states, "Paul disembarked in the port of Tyre, where he spent seven days with a group of disciples who, according to Acts 21:4, told Paul 'through the Spirit, that he should not go up to Jerusalem.' Ignoring this clear divine prohibition, he continued his journey to Jerusalem, giving evidence that by then 'something' was working in him that prodded, coerced or drove him to go. In all honesty we ought to ask ourselves, what was the source of this compulsive behavior? If the Holy Spirit was compelling him to undertake this trip (as most Bible scholars affirm), then why so many misgivings and prohibitions? Does God contradict himself? (2 Tim. 2:13)."

Paul arrived in Jerusalem and told James and the elders what things God had wrought among the Gentiles by his ministry (Acts 21:19). The conversation then changed, with James telling him the concern of the believing Jews who were zealous of the Law. Paul was accused by some of teaching the Jews to depart from the Law. This, of course, was not true. Paul was encouraged by James to shave his head and purify himself, according to the Law, with four men who had taken a vow (Acts 21:20–26). Paul yielded and entered the temple to make an offering to signify the days of purification. The Jews who were of Asia saw Paul in the temple and stirred up the people to lay hands on Paul by accusing him of teaching against the Law (Acts 21:27–31). Paul was almost killed by this mob.

By going to Jerusalem, Paul placed himself in a no-win situation. If he refused the request of James and the elders, he would have been accused of not honoring the Law. James and the other apostles were called to the Jews. They had a legitimate concern and tried to work out a strategy to reach the Jews. Paul, however, was called to the Gentiles. He placed himself in a dangerous situation by yielding to the request of James. He submitted to a legalistic requirement in order to appease legalistic believers.

This was totally contrary to everything Paul preached to the Gentiles. Norman Parrish states:

> By blindly accepting and carrying out the "sound advice" of James and the elders, Paul virtually reverted to Judaism, becoming a "transgressor" according to his own words in Galatians 2:18. By not submitting to the Holy Spirit and to the legitimate spiritual authority of his peers (such as Phillip and Agabus) and his traveling companions (Trophimus and Luke, among many others), Paul ended up submitting to the doubtful authority of James and the elders, considered the main representatives of the most legalistic and sectarian wing of the first century church.

Paul ended up in chains. He eventually appealed to Caesar. This means that he could not be freed but had to go to Rome. He encountered a storm on the way to Rome and survived the shipwreck. He finally arrived in Rome. He spent two years in a hired house as a prisoner (Acts 28:30). He ministered to all who came to him. This is the way the Book of Acts ends. Paul's public ministry ended while he was in prison. He did not have the freedom to travel. He did not have the freedom to plant and establish churches. He did not have the freedom to visit the churches he had established.

He wrote letters from prison to speak to the churches. Earlier, Paul had desired to go to Rome and then to Spain. He finally got to Rome, but there is no record of him ever going to Spain. (See Romans 1:13, 15; 15:28.) He ended up in Rome, and died there.

Ralph Mahoney states, "In Galatians 2:7, Paul wrote that the gospel of the circumcision (Gentiles) was committed to him. He was the apostle to the Gentiles and what's more he knew it. Paul knew what God's vision was for his life in very clear terms.... I believe Paul could have lived much more of his life in freedom if he stayed within the limits of God's vision, if he had concentrated on his work among the Gentiles." By going to Jerusalem, Paul was bound and delivered into the hands of the Gentiles (Acts 21:11). He would end up with the Gentiles (his calling) one way or another (free or bound).

> Wherefore we would have come unto you, even I Paul, once and again; but Satan hindered us.
>
> —1 THESSALONIANS 2:18

This verse shows us that Satan is actively involved in hindering apostolic ministries. Paul was a target of Satan. Paul was the most influential apostle to the Gentiles in the early church, and he was aware of this activity to block and sidetrack him in his ministry.

I am not assuming that God's will was not fulfilled in Paul's life. He did testify in Rome, which was the capital of the empire. The Lord protected Paul in spite of his decisions, but I believe that Paul could have gone to Rome another way. He could have been free for more time to minister to the church. Satan tried to hinder and thwart the plan of God in this great apostle's ministry.

2. Pride

And lest I should be exalted above measure through the abundance of the revelations, there was given to me a thorn in the flesh, the messenger of Satan to buffet me, lest I should be exalted above measure.

—2 Corinthians 12:7

Pride goeth before destruction, and an haughty spirit before a fall.

—Proverbs 16:18

The apostolic ministry is a ministry of revelation. Apostles are stewards of the mysteries of God (1 Cor. 4:1). This revelatory anointing helps the church understand the things that have been hidden in previous ages (Eph. 3:1–5). Different apostles will operate in different levels of revelation. Paul had more revelation than many of the apostles. Because of the abundance of revelation given to him, there was a danger of him being lifted up in pride. God allowed a messenger of Satan to buffet him.

> Apostles must stay on course and finish what they have been sent to do. They must stay on course with their doctrine and lifestyle. They cannot allow revelation or success to open the door for Leviathan to operate in their ministries.

The word *messenger* is the same as *angel*. I believe this was an evil angel that opposed Paul's ministry, stirring up trouble wherever Paul went. God allowed this to keep Paul in a place of dependency and humility. Paul's tendency would have been to be exalted (prideful) because of the abundance of revelation given to him.

There is a danger of apostles operating in pride due to the revelation they receive and minister with. Pride can lead to destruction and a fall. Pride and arrogance are major pitfalls of the apostolic ministry. Apostles can have tremendous breakthroughs, which can lead to boasting. As in the case of Paul, God allows opposition to come to some apostles to keep them in a place of dependence and humility.

Pride is a demon that works with stubbornness, vanity, and self-will. Apostles are sent ones. They should be completely dependent upon the Sender. There is no place for pride or independence. Satan will attempt to cause any ministry gift to become puffed up, especially that of apostles. Pride can open the way for destruction. Satan delights in destroying ministry gifts, including apostles.

Many supporting spirits work with pride. Leviathan is the king of pride (Job 41:34). Job 41 gives a description of this creature known as Leviathan. He is referred to as a large sea serpent (Isa. 27:1). Some translations refer to him as "the crocodile." He is called a crooked serpent. The word *crooked* means "twisted or perverted." Leviathan is a spirit that attempts to attack ministries, especially apostolic ministries. He is a ruling spirit that dwells in the sea. The sea is symbolic of the nations.

Pride can twist or pervert leaders from their true calling and destiny. Pride can cause leaders to go astray from the vision given to them by the Lord. Apostles must stay on course and finish what they have been sent to do. They must stay on course with their doctrine and lifestyle. They cannot allow revelation or success to open the door for Leviathan to operate in their ministries.

Apostles are servants. They must serve in humility. They are not to be worshiped or exalted above measure. They do not take the place of Jesus.

Manifestations of Leviathan include haughtiness, vanity, arrogance, anger, control, domination, covenant breaking (Job 41:4), strife, hardness of heart (v. 24), stubbornness (v. 22), resistance to change and new things, and deception. Leviathan can cause leaders to be closed to the counsel of others (v. 15). Pride can blind leaders to truth and cause them to operate in behavior that is destructive to their callings and ministries. Pride works with the spirit of destruction. Destruction can destroy ministries, families, marriages, churches, and nations. Apostolic ministries that go astray can bring much damage to the lives of people.

We cannot think of men more highly than we ought to think of them. Apostles are servants. They must serve in humility. They are not to be worshiped or exalted above measure. They do not take the place of Jesus. Jesus is the Head of the church. Apostles are servants under the headship of the Lord.

Apostles must be willing to submit to the other ministry gifts. Although they are set in the church *first,* they must accept and work with the other ministry gifts. Elders are to submit one to another (1 Pet. 5:5). There is mutual submission among the gifts, although there is ranking and authority that is recognized. This is why team ministry is so important. Apostles who state, "I'm an apostle, and I don't need to listen to anyone except God," are dangerous. This is a manifestation of pride that will eventually lead to a downfall.

Apostles must not turn their churches and ministries into a personal kingdom. They must avoid becoming sectarian and exclusive. Paul rebuked the Corinthian church for its sectarian attitude. This was the result of carnality. Apostles who become sectarian and divisive are operating in the flesh. This grieves the Holy Spirit and is another manifestation of pride. Apostles are given to the church as a gift for the perfecting of the saints. The church is not given to apostles to build their own kingdom. The people of God do not belong to the apostle, but they belong to the Lord.

Apostles must not use their authority for destruction but for edification. Apostles have been given authority to edify (build) the church, not destroy it. When the behavior of an apostle becomes destructive, God will remove that apostle. Apostles who operate in pride often become controlling and dominating. When this happens, they are using their authority for destruction and not for edification (2 Cor. 13:10).

Apostles must not turn their churches and ministries into a personal kingdom. They must avoid becoming sectarian and exclusive.

We have dealt with leaders who *curse* people for leaving their churches. This is a sign of control and witchcraft. Apostles are not to have dominion over our faith (2 Cor. 1:24). Paul did exercise authority in the case of an unrepentant man in the Corinthian church. He turned him over to Satan for the destruction of his flesh. Apostles do have authority to deal with sin and rebellion. Leaders who curse people for leaving local churches cannot use the example of Paul. Apostles who manifest anger in cursing people are often operating in pride and control.

> But Hezekiah rendered not again according to the benefit done unto him; for his heart was lifted up: therefore there was wrath upon him, and upon Judah and Jerusalem.
> —2 Chronicles 32:25

Old Testament kings are types of the apostolic ministry. One of the failures of some of these kings was in the area of pride. Hezekiah was a godly king. God blessed him with fame, riches, and honor. Hezekiah allowed pride to enter his heart during the end of his life. One of the manifestations of his pride was in showing the ambassadors from Babylon all of his treasures (Isa. 39). The good news is that Hezekiah humbled himself before his death (2 Chron. 32:26).

Amaziah was a godly king whom fell into the sin of pride. He refused to listen to the voice of the prophet who brought him correction (2 Chron. 25:16). His pride led him into idolatry (2 Chron. 25:14).

> But when he was strong, his heart was lifted up to his destruction…
>
> —2 CHRONICLES 26:16

Amaziah's son, Uzziah, also fell into the sin of pride. His pride led him to transgress God's commandment concerning the priesthood. He was smitten with leprosy as he burned incense in the sanctuary. Uzziah died a leper.

Apostles must be careful when they become established and strong. Success can make a leader vulnerable to pride. Many of these kings started with humble hearts, but they allowed pride to cause them to go astray.

> The pride of thine heart hath deceived thee…
>
> —OBADIAH 1:3

Pride can open the door for deception. Deceiving spirits can lead apostles to preach doctrines that are contrary to the Word of God. Apostles must remain sound in doctrine. They cannot allow personal doctrines that have no scriptural basis to affect their preaching and teaching.

3. COVETOUSNESS

> And he said unto them, Take heed, and beware of covetousness: for a man's life consisteth not in the abundance of the things which he possesseth.
>
> —LUKE 12:15

> Ye cannot serve God and mammon.
>
> —LUKE 16:13

Jesus warned the apostles about covetousness. Covetousness is idolatry (Col. 3:5). Many Old Testament kings, who were types of apostles, were guilty of idolatry. The counterpart in the New Testament is a leader who is guilty of covetousness. Apostles cannot allow themselves to be controlled by the spirit of mammon.

Mammon is a ruling spirit that controls money. Mammon works with spirits of greed, selfishness, covetousness, and materialism. Jesus said that we cannot serve God and mammon. This means that mammon can take the place of God. This again is idolatry.

Mammon attempts to control churches and ministries. When decisions are based on money instead of the Holy Spirit, the spirit of mammon is in control. Mammon will attempt to control and influence apostolic ministries.

A lack of money will not stop apostles from ministering. They will know how to operate in abundance and suffer need when necessary.

Apostles can fall into the pitfall of covetousness because they have a grace in the area of money. The believers in the early church willingly came and laid money at the apostles' feet. They did so willingly because great grace was upon them. There is a spirit of giving in apostolic churches. Apostles have a resource anointing and are able to release large amounts of money into the kingdom. If an apostle is not careful, the enemy can use this as a trap to ensnare him with/into covetousness.

The motivation for an apostle must not be money. Apostles must be motivated by their commission. Apostles must know how to abase and abound. In other words, a lack of money will not stop them from ministering. They will know how to operate in abundance and suffer need when necessary. This is what gives them the ability to overcome in different situations. The church should support apostolic ministries, but apostles cannot greedily demand maintenance. Integrity in the area of money is an important part of the apostle's ministry.

Paul supported himself and would not receive financial support from the Corinthian church. He did this in order to separate himself from false apostles. Paul did receive support from the Philippian church. He wanted fruit to abound to their accounts. Apostles are concerned about the people being blessed, so they will encourage them to give. This is to be their motivation, not greed or covetousness.

> For neither at any time used we flattering words, as ye know, nor a cloke of covetousness; God is witness: Nor of men sought we glory, neither of you, nor yet of others, when we might have been burdensome, as the apostles of Christ.
>
> —1 THESSALONIANS 2:5–6

This is Paul's description of his apostolic team. They did not come with flattering words as a pretense for covetousness. They did not come to be a burden. Apostolic ministry must never become a financial burden to the church. They must not place heavy responsibilities and financial constraints upon the people of God. Covetousness will cause leadership to drive and demand greedily from the church. When that happens, the ministry becomes a burden instead of a blessing.

4. ABUSE *of* AUTHORITY

> Therefore I write these things being absent, lest being present I should use sharpness, according to the power which the Lord hath given me to edification, and not to destruction.
>
> —2 CORINTHIANS 13:10

Authority is one of the marks of true apostolic ministry. This authority is given for edification and not for destruction. All authority comes from God. God entrusts apostles with tremendous authority. They must be careful not to abuse it.

Paul defended his apostolic authority in the second epistle to the Corinthians. Paul understood that his authority was given for edification and not for destruction. This means that authority, if misused, can bring destruction.

God does not give men authority for personal use. When leaders use authority for personal agendas, they are guilty of abusing authority. This is also true when leaders use the authority given to them to control and dominate God's people.

> Then Asa was wroth with the seer, and put him in a prison house; for he was in a rage with him because of this thing. And Asa oppressed some of the people the same time.
> —2 Chronicles 16:10

The king used his authority to oppress some of the people. He was angry with the prophet and had him put in prison. Asa was a godly king who fell into the pitfall of pride toward the end of his reign. He made a covenant with an ungodly king and was rebuked by the prophet. Instead of humbling himself, he manifested anger and pride and abused his kingly authority. Misused authority will cause apostles to oppress people instead of building them up and releasing them. Apostles are not to be spiritual dictators. They are to use their authority for edification.

> What is my reward then? Verily that, when I preach the gospel, I may make the gospel of Christ without charge, that I abuse not my power in the gospel.
> —1 Corinthians 9:18

> Neither shall he multiply wives to himself, that his heart turn not away: neither shall he greatly multiply to himself silver and gold.
> —Deuteronomy 17:17

Apostles have a right to receive financial support. They must be careful not to abuse this right. Apostolic authority is not given for financial gain. When leaders use their authority to take advantage of people financially, this is an abuse of authority.

The king was not to use his position to multiply wives, silver, and gold unto himself. He was not to use his position to benefit himself. The king was not to use his position to multiply his power and wealth, which would be an abuse of authority. God will bless faithfulness.

There has always been a temptation for leaders to use their position and influence for their own benefit. Apostles have a responsibility to use the authority given to them in the right way. Unto whom much is given, much is required. The more power and influence a person has, the more they must avoid using it for personal gain.

Apostles are not infallible. Apostles are human and susceptible to mistakes. They must guard against the pitfalls of pride, covetousness, self-will, and control. Apostles must develop the character of humility and holiness. Most importantly, they must have the attitude and the heart of a servant.

Apostles have been chosen to serve the church and the world. They must never abuse their authority. God is sending many apostles. Many are now being trained and developed in the area of character. The church will be blessed as it receives these emerging ministries. Let us pray for discernment and scriptural wisdom to receive and test those who claim to be apostles.

BIBLIOGRAPHY

Beck, William F., *et al. The Holy Bible in the Language of Today, An American Translation*. New Haven, MI: Leader Publishing Co., 1976.

Butler, Trent C. *Holman Bible Dictionary*. Nashville, TN: Broadman and Holman Publishers, 1991.

Cannistraci, David. Apostles and the Emerging Apostolic Movement. Ventura, CA: Gospel Light Publications, 1996.

Cartledge, David. *The Apostolic Revolution*. Chester Hill, Australia: Paraclete Institute, 2000.

Conybeare, W. J., and J. S. Howson. *The Life and Epistles of St. Paul*. Grand Rapids, MI: Wm. B. Eerdmans Publishing Company, 1978.

Cooke, Graham. *A Divine Confrontation*. Shippensburg, PA: Destiny Image, 1999.

Coombs, Barney. *Apostles Today*. Kent, England: Sovereign World Ltd., 1996.

David, Jonathan. *Apostolic Strategies Affecting Nations*. n.p.: self-published, 1997.

Eberle, Harold. *The Complete Wineskin*. Yakima, WA: Winepress Publishing, 1993.

Eckhardt, John. *Apostolic Ministry*. n.p.: n.d.

———. *Fifty Truths Concerning Apostolic Ministry*. n.p.: Crusaders Ministries, 1994.

————. *Moving in the Apostolic.* n.p.: Renew, 1999.

————. *Presbyteries and Apostolic Teams.* n.p.: Crusaders Ministries, 2000.

————. *The Apostolic Church.* n.p.: Crusaders Ministries, 1996.

————. *The Ministry Anointing of the Apostle.* n.p.: Crusaders Ministries, 1993.

Gentile, Ernest B. *Your Sons and Daughters Shall Prophesy: Prophetic Gifts in Ministry Today.* Ada, MI: Chosen Books, 1999.

Goodspeed, Edgar J., and J. M. Powis Smith, eds. *The Bible: An American Translation.* Chicago: University of Chicago Press, 1931; 2nd edition, 1935.

Hamon, Bill. *Prophets, Pitfalls and Principles.* Shippensburg, PA: Destiny Image, 2001.

Jones, Bryn. *The Radical Church.* Shippensburg, PA: Destiny Image, 1999.

Knox, Ronald A., trans. *The New Testament of Our Lord and Saviour Jesus Christ—Newly Translated from the Latin Vulgate and Authorized by the Archbishops and Bishops of England and Wales.* n.p.: Burns Oates and Washbourne Ltd., 1948.

Lyne, Peter. *First Apostles Last Apostles.* n.p.: Sovereign World, 1999.

Moffatt, James. *A New Translation of the Bible, Containing the Old and New Testaments.* New York: Doran, 1926. Revised edition, New York: Harper and Brothers, 1935. Reprinted, Grand Rapids: Kregel, 1995.

Montgomery, Helen Barrett. *The New Testament in Modern*

English, Centenary Translation. Philadelphia, PA: The Judson Press, 1952.

Nee, Watchman. *The Normal Christian Church Life.* Anaheim, CA: Living Stream Ministry, 1980.

Price, Frederick K. C. *Integrity: The Guarantee for Success.* n.p.: Dr. Frederick K. C. Price Ministries, 2000.

Prince, Derek. *Apostles and Shepherds* Tape Series. Ft. Lauderdale, FL: Derek Prince Ministries, n.d.

———. *Apostolic Teams.* Tape Series. Ft. Lauderdale, FL: Derek Prince Ministries: n.d.

Rotherham, Joseph Bryant. *The New Testament.* London: Samuel Bagster and Sons, 1872.

Sapp, Roger. *The Last Apostles on Earth.* Shippensburg, PA: Companion Press, 1995.

Spurrell, Helen. *A Translation of the Old Testament Scriptures from the Original Hebrew.* Grand Rapids, MI: Kregel Publications, 1987.

St. Irenaeus. *Against Heresies. The Gnosis Archive.* www.gnosis.org/library/advh1.htm (accessed April 28, 2010).

Strauch, Alexander. *Biblical Eldership.* Littleton, CO: Lewis and Roth Publishers, n.d. http://www.peacemakers.net/resources/strauch/biblicaleldership.htm (accessed August 17, 2010).

Tertullian. *On the "Prescription" of Heretics. The Tertullian Project.* http://www.tertullian.org/articles/bindley_test/bindley_test_07prae.htm (accessed April 28, 2010).

The Twentieth Century New Testament. A Translation Into Modern English. Made From the Original Greek. New York, NY:

Fleming H. Revell Co., 1902. Revised 1904.

Vaughan, Curtis, ed. *The Word: The Bible From 26 Translations.* Grand Rapids, MI: Baker Publishing Group, 1998.

Vine, W. E. *Vine's Complete Expository Dictionary of Old and New Testament Words.* Nashville, TN: Thomas Nelson, 1985.

Wagner, C. Peter. *Apostles and Prophets.* Ventura, CA: Regal Books, 2000.

Weymouth, Richard Francis. *New Testament In Modern Speech.* Grand Rapids, MI: Kregel Publications, 1978.

Williams, Charles B. *The New Testament in the Language of the People.* Chicago, IL: Moody Press, 1937.

Wuest, Kenneth S. *The New Testament: An Expanded Translation.* Grand Rapids, MI: Wm. B. Eerdmans, 1961, 1994.

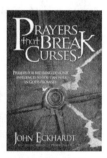
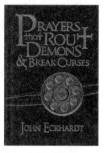

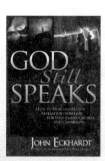